When Spirits Walk

Jacquelyn Procter Gray

Illustrated
by
Leslie E. Gray

Bloomington, IN   Milton Keynes, UK

authorHOUSE®

AuthorHouse™
1663 Liberty Drive, Suite 200
Bloomington, IN 47403
www.authorhouse.com
Phone: 1-800-839-8640

AuthorHouse™ UK Ltd.
500 Avebury Boulevard
Central Milton Keynes, MK9 2BE
www.authorhouse.co.uk
Phone: 08001974150

First published by AuthorHouse 9/5/2006

ISBN: 1-4259-5340-9 (sc)

*Printed in the United States of America
Bloomington, Indiana*

This book is printed on acid-free paper.

Acknowledgements

I have many people to thank for helping me complete this book. Chuck and Jo Shaffer of *Old Tennessee Valley Magazine* began publishing my ghost stories for their Halloween edition and have graciously welcomed me as a permanent part of their fabulous "magazine family." I owe them immeasurable credit for their guidance and lessons, and I am proud to be part of such an outstanding publication.

Ranee' Pruitt, Jim Maples, Linda Maples, and Robert Reeves have given me advice and suggestions, and spent many long hours with me discussing strategy over sangria and cheap wine.

The outstanding cover was designed by Jim, Linda, and Ranee' and the photograph of my daughter Leslie Gray, aka the ghost of Sally Carter, was taken by Linda Maples at the annual Maple Hill Cemetery Stroll.

Ranee' Pruitt, archivist at the Huntsville/Madison

County Public Library, gathered the creepy old photographs from the library files and suggested several of the stories in this book. The old house on the cover is that of "Cedarhurst," the home haunted by Sally Carter. Many thanks to Ranee' as well as the Huntsville/Madison County Public Library and all who have made it an outstanding repository of historic information that it is today.

Robert Reeves nagged me daily to get this finished and drove Ranee' and me to many of the old sites where these stories occurred. Without his encouragement, I would still be talking about writing this book years from now.

My brother Donnell Procter is constantly on the lookout for interesting stories for me to write. He is responsible for some of these as well.

I also want to thank my daughter Leslie Gray, who joined in our late night discussions (without the wine) for sharing her talent in drawing the illustrations in this book. Unlike most teenagers, Leslie has always been enthusiastic about the unusual things in which I enlist her help. Her portrayal as Sally Carter has landed her some interesting television and speaking gigs. I'm very grateful to have a child who shares my love of history.

Dedicated with love to Leslie and Jeff

Introduction

Whether you believe in ghosts, don't believe, or are not sure, almost everyone enjoys hearing ghost stories. We humans are most alive when we are frightened, and don't we all love a good mystery? I will not try to sway anyone's belief in ghosts, but it is important for the reader to know that none of these incidents were fabricated in my imagination. These stories are based on historical research, and if a story has been told but cannot be authenticated, I have indicated that as well.

I have interviewed several people who have witnessed these occurrences, and in two stories, I have been a witness myself. I only regret that there are so many other tales that I will not tell to protect the homes or site of the ghostly encounters. Perhaps one day....

Table of Contents

Cedarhurst, home of Sally Carter
Photo courtesy of the Huntsville Public Library

The Ghost of Sally Carter

For generations, teenagers in Huntsville, Alabama have camped out at the gravesite of Sally Carter, the 16-year-old from Virginia who died mysteriously while visiting her sister in 1837. The search for Sally's ghost was a rite of passage in the cemetery near the plantation once known as Cedarhurst. Ah, but Sally was an elusive ghost. At times the cowering teens would see a floating blue light, an orb in the darkness as if Sally was playing with them. Some claimed to hear Sally singing softly in the dead of night, while others went away disappointed that Sally did not appear, yet pleased to say that they too were among the many who had gone in search of the elusive ghost.

The legend of Sally's ghost was not concocted from the imagination of a teen with a flair for drama. Oh no! Sally's ghost has been seen for some time since a terrible thunderstorm that hit Huntsville in the early

1900s. But to fully appreciate the wanderings of Sally's spirit, it is important to first know her story.

Stephen Ewing and his wife were born in Russell County, Virginia. They moved to north Alabama some time in the early 1800s when wealthy planters from all over came to grow cotton in the paradise of the Tennessee Valley. Ewing became the director of the State National Bank of Alabama and commissioner of the Indian Creek Navigation Company, which had financed the development of a canal from the Big Spring in Huntsville to the Tennessee River in Triana. The Indian Creek Canal provided a way for plantation owners to send their cotton bales, after prices had been brokered on Cotton Row, by barge to the Tennessee River to be shipped to other ports. In addition, Ewing owned and operated several plantations.

The Ewing plantation known as Cedarhurst was built on present-day Whitesburg Drive, the old time route from downtown Huntsville to Ditto's Landing. The Ewings' home was a traditional plantation-style with high ceilings, formal rooms for entertaining guests, sleeping rooms upstairs, and of course, massive columns in front. The many slaves were quartered out back.

The family grew to include nine children, and the house grew as well. Modern historians learned that differences in the wall thickness indicated that it was built in at least two different phases. A school was built near the house for their children and those in the vicinity. The refinement of Virginia was brought to Alabama!

In 1837, Mrs. Ewing's sister Sally Carter came to visit. Their father, who had served in the American Revolution, was a widower with seven children. The three younger children had been sent to be raised by Samuel Carter. Mr. Carter had died in 1828, leaving the young children orphaned. Sixteen-year-old Sally would be a help to her older sister and a playmate for her young nieces and nephews.

The good times were not meant to be. Sally died of an unknown illness not long after her arrival at Cedarhurst. During her illness, she stayed in one of the upstairs bedrooms, and to keep Sally ever near, she was buried in the plantation cemetery under a

Sally Carter's ghost

3

tree. On her headstone were inscribed the words, "My flesh shall slumber in the ground, Till the last trumpet's joyful sound. Then burst the chains with sweet surprise, And in my savior's image rise."

Not long after that, three of the Ewing children died of the deadly whooping cough, and were buried next to their beloved Aunt Sally.

To lose so many young ones was tragic, yet common in those days before vaccinations. Some families left for the country when news of an epidemic was at hand, but many times the disease struck and killed their victims only hours after the symptoms first appeared.

Sally's sister, Mrs. Ewing, died 12 years later at age 53. She had lived a relatively long life in comparison to the others. She too was buried in the nearby cemetery.

The year 1861 brought another tragedy, this time to the whole country. The Civil War left many people destitute and impoverished. Though Stephen Ewing had been a very wealthy man, he lost much of his fortune too. In 1865, he sold out for $7,000 and moved to Aberdeen, Mississippi to be near his grandchildren. He died soon after and was buried in the Oddfellows Rest Cemetery.

The story would seem to end there had it not been for an event which seemed to draw Sally back to the place of her death, where some say she remains today.

After the Thornton family bought the house in 1919, they had visitors from south Alabama. Because there were so many people staying over, the 17-year-old cousin slept in a cot just outside the bedroom where Sally had died. During the night, a thunderstorm moved in with high winds and bright flashes of lightning. Explosions of thunder filled the sky and rattled the delicate windowpanes. Nature's fury had visited the small plantation graveyard as well.

The young man was missing the next morning. After a search, they discovered him on the front porch, trembling with fear. The stunned family members listened to the incredible story he had to tell. During the night, at the height of the storm, the young man had been awakened. He opened his eyes and saw before him, the shadowy figure of a young girl, about his own age. The young girl told him that her headstone had been blown over in the storm, and she wanted him to put it back in its place, over her grave. And then she vanished. The startled young man was so upset and in his confusion, he somehow ended up on the porch, where he was found a few hours later.

When the host family and his relatives went down to the graveyard, they confirmed the story the ghost had told – her headstone had been knocked over during the storm. The young man and his family hastily left town, but the headstone was never uprighted.

Over the next few years, there were many more sightings of the ghostly Sally Carter. On one occasion, a visitor who was upstairs, saw Sally coming up the front staircase toward her. The visitor quickly launched down the back stairs and reported the sighting to her hostess. "Oh, it was only Sally," was the unsurprised reply.

Another woman who lived in the house at one time was building a fire in the downstairs fireplace one night. Her small baby was upstairs asleep in what was known as Sally's room. She heard someone walking up the stairs and she quickly went to investigate. Her baby was sleeping soundly and no one else was around. On another occasion, she heard the hall door open and close three times in quick succession.

At some point, the owners of the home took in renters. The man who lived in Sally's room was a smoker, and apparently the ethereal Sally objected. Heavy glass ashtrays were tossed into the air and fell to the floor, shattered. Although the renter kept the door bolted from the inside, it was not uncommon for him to discover that it had been unbolted, by someone else, on several occasions.

In 1985, new life was breathed into the old plantation house when it was transformed into a Decorators' Show House for the public to see. It was a chance for local decorators to showcase their talents and the admission that was charged would be donated to charity. Sally's room was transformed into a teenager's dream come true. Apparently however, it wasn't exactly Sally's dream, and her displeasure was soon apparent. The room was bright and alive. During the time that the house was open to the public, volunteers would come in to find that Sally's room had been tossed during the night. Flowers were turned over, a diary was thrown onto the floor and the bedding was wadded up. It looked as if someone, perhaps Sally, had thrown a fit.

It was at about this time that Cedarhurst had been transformed into an upscale subdivision. Although the plantation home remained at the center of the new project and became the clubhouse, expensive new homes and a security wall sprang up around it. It was time that the bodies in the small cemetery be moved as well. For the teenagers who visited the grave of Sally Carter, it was the end of an era. But Sally's headstone was already gone.

Over the years, souvenir hunters had chipped away at Sally's headstone. According to a local historian, a disturbed young man went to Sally's grave one night and demanded that she appear before him. In a fit of rage, he took a sledgehammer to her headstone, smashing it into little pieces.

The graves were reinterred at Maple Hill Cemetery. While workers found the vault that contained the grave of Mrs. Ewing, the coffin was gone. There was no vault or coffin found in Sally's grave. Buckets of dirt, presumably the dust that had once been mortal bodies, were buried in unmarked graves at Maple Hill. The location of these graves are known to only a few people, and will never be made public so as not to invite potentially destructive trespassers. Sally Carter and her family are finally left alone in death, though her ghost continues to haunt the last home she ever knew.

Unlucky in Love – The Ghost of Hazel Green

In a cotton field near Hazel Green, Alabama, a stand of trees obscures an ancient Indian mound. At one time, a large home stood on the highest point of the Indian mound, overlooking the highway between Fayetteville and Huntsville, as well as the fertile cotton fields that surrounded it. It was a fine home, and travelers were invited to stay there for a night or two. The woman who lived there was notoriously beautiful. Elizabeth Dale had auburn hair, dark eyes and a fair complexion. Still, the poor woman had terrible luck with men. Every time she married someone, he died.

Elizabeth would be described in modern times as a "serial widow." Six husbands died, and the mysterious nature of their deaths raised the suspicions of people all around. She was accused of killing her husbands, and some even said she used rat poison. Were the spirits of ancient Indians angry that their sacred ceremonial ground was desecrated by the white people who lived upon it? Who is to say what caused the deaths of her unfortunate husbands? The answers went to the grave with the beautiful Elizabeth.

Home of the Black Widow of Hazel Green
Photo courtesy of the Huntsville Public Library

Elizabeth was one of 10 children born to Adam Dale and Mary "Polly" Hall. Adam Dale received land grants in Tennessee for his service in the Revolutionary War. In 1790, he married 18 year-old Polly from Sussex County, Delaware. In 1797, they left Maryland to settle in Liberty, Dekalb County, Tennessee, traveling through eastern Tennessee and the Cumberland

Mountain Range. They were the first settlers in Dekalb County. Daughter Elizabeth Evans Dale was a very young child at this time, having been born October 28, 1795 in Worchester County, Maryland.

In 1812, Adam Dale fought under General Andrew Jackson at the Battle of Horseshoe Bend. He is credited for having raised, equipped, and commanded a company of 100 volunteers from Smith, Tennessee, also in Dekalb County. His company camped near a large spring near a small Alabama community called Meridianville. They were just eight miles north of Huntsville and near the future home of his daughter, Elizabeth.

It was also in 1812 when 17-year-old Elizabeth married 20-year-old Samuel Gibbons, who was or became a Baptist minister. After 18 years of marriage, Samuel Gibbons contracted black tongue. He died on June 14, 1830, leaving Elizabeth a widow for the first time at age 35. Elizabeth then moved to Columbia, Tennessee to be near her brother Edward W. Dale, a prominent citizen of that area. Unfortunately, he committed suicide after trouble at his bank.

Elizabeth remarried fifteen months after her husband's death. Certainly no one was surprised. Men found her appealing and charming. Elizabeth was known to be fond of horses and expensive clothing.

Phillip Flanagan, Elizabeth's new husband, was 35-

years-old. Their marriage took place on October 3, 1831, but he survived only six months after the wedding. He died on March 14, 1832 and was buried at Maple Hill Cemetery in Huntsville, Alabama.

Nearly nineteen months later, Elizabeth married her third husband, Alexander Jeffries. She was 38 and he was 60 when they exchanged vows on November 6, 1833. Mr. Jeffries owned a plantation near Hazel Green, Alabama and married Elizabeth eight years after his first wife died.

Hazel Green, Alabama is a community four miles from the Tennessee border. By 1809, it consisted of several stores, two hotels, and several grocery stores. It grew quickly, and by 1821 when the town was incorporated, there were three to four hundred settlers within the city. Hazel Green was a popular resting place for people traveling between Huntsville and Fayetteville, and it was near the Meridian Pike where Alexander Jeffries chose to live.

Jeffries had bought his plantation in 1817 from Archibald Patterson for $1,800. The next year, he bought additional property from Thomas Murphy for $700. He cleared the land and planted cotton, which was well-suited to that area. He bought slaves as he needed them.

The Jeffries home was built over sacred Indian

ground. The locals wondered aloud why they would tempt fate by building on an Indian Mound. Located one mile east of Hazel Green, it was situated so that Alexander had a sweeping view of the country around the spacious log cabin that was his home. Even with such a wondrous view, the site was strangely spooky. One source claims it consisted of four rooms, while another claimed only two.

This was to be the new home of Elizabeth Dale. The couple had two children: William, who was born in 1834 when Elizabeth was 39, and Mary Elizabeth, who was born in 1837 when Elizabeth was 42.

By February 1838, Alexander Jeffries was not in good health. He called his good friend and neighbor, Abner Tate, to witness his will. His will provided for his older children from his first wife, while the rest went to Elizabeth and their two children. The will stated that he was of sound mind, though his health was bad.

Seven months later, on September 14, 1838, Alexander Jeffries died at age 65. He was laid to rest in the nearby family cemetery in the shade of holly trees. Next to him was his first wife, Frances, who had died 13 years earlier. Few people knew of Elizabeth's earlier marriages, and blamed the death of Alexander on angry Indian spirits.

Eight months after Alexander Jeffries died, 44-year-old Elizabeth married again on May 15, 1839. Justice of the Peace J. H. Pierce performed the wedding between Elizabeth Jeffries and Robert High, who was about 39-years-old. Robert High was well-acquainted with marriage too. Elizabeth was his fourth wife and he had a 17-year-old son named Henry Albert High. The newlyweds lived in Elizabeth's home in Hazel Green.

Husband number four, Robert High, was a native of North Carolina. He was restless, considered to be a dashing widower in the Tuscaloosa social scene, but went to great pains to cover his bald head. He served as a representative in the State legislature during 1838 and 1839, but spent too much time in the lobby eating apples and peanuts. Unfortunately, but to no one's surprise, he was defeated in the next election.

Just three years after their wedding, Robert High died in 1841, broke and without a will.

To the townspeople, four dead husbands were just too much to accept and she was running out of friends. To complicate matters, Elizabeth was already having problems with her neighbor, Abner Tate. Court records show that Elizabeth sued Abner Tate and Jacob H. Pierce for $1,400.00, claiming that they owed her for the cotton crop of 1840. In 1843, Pierce wrote to Elizabeth:

"Madam, in the name of God, do you intend to try to ruin me? When I have protected your interest ever since the death of your late husband, Alexander Jeffries, in thousands of instances. Lest your mind should be treacherous, I will name a few. After the death of Mr. Jeffries, when his children should have been your friends, but instead of that, they were your most inveterate enemies and even went so far as to say you were the cause of his death, which was reported from one end of this country to the other. Who were your friends?"

Her reply was surprisingly pleasant and somewhat off the subject: "I received your letter by father late on Friday evening, and company came in just at that time, so I had no time to write until I got home from church this afternoon. I am sorry to find your feelings are hurt with me, for I never intended to say or do anything to hurt you in any respect. Your kindness to me I do esteem in the highest, and ever shall, for I always have believed you to be my friend, and you may rest assured that I will not nor never intend to sue you..."

She later wrote, "I intended to have sent this last evening, but on account of Mary E. having a chill at church, it detained me so that when I was done writing, it was too late to send it. Then I thought I would get father to hand it to you in Huntsville, but finding you will be at home today, I will send it there. I hope all will be well yet. 1 am your friend...."

On August 13, 1844, Elizabeth's daughter Mary

died at age 7. Surely her death was attributed to natural causes! Or was it?

Elizabeth waited four years after Robert High's death before marrying again. She married again in 1845 at the age of 51. Her new husband, Absalom Brown, was 52.

Elizabeth Dale Gibbons Flanagan Jeffries High Brown and her new husband built an impressive plantation house on the property purchased by husband number three, Alexander Jeffries. The home, which faced the east, consisted of eight large rooms, four upstairs and four downstairs. There were two stairways and a huge main door of two panels bordered with tiny panes of glass. Built on the site of a former two-story log cabin built by the late Alexander Jeffries, it was still on an Indian mound overlooking the cotton fields. One source referred to it as Pleasant Mound. It was richly furnished and even had servants' bells in every room. In spite of the beautiful and expensive furniture, Elizabeth wanted tall mirrors and costly mantle-pieces, though she was never able to acquire them.

The road to Hazel Green ran just a few feet from the north side of the home and intersected a few hundred yards to the front of the house with a lane which was bordered by approximately a dozen slave cottages.

Even the landscaping was magnificent. A row of tall

cedars and pines around the hill circled beds of all kinds of flowers and shrubs. Boar grass was planted along the main walk in front, and the brick walks leading to the stables and icehouse were lined with shrubbery.

It took over a year for a carpenter and slave to build the 8-room L-shaped mansion, and it became the center for festive parties. But the splendor and gaiety of the Brown plantation came to an end on a night in 1847. Only a year after the marriage, Absalom Brown died of a strange malady, a slow and painful death.

The cause of death was unknown. The unexplained illness was described as "a malady which caused fast and terrific swelling of his body." Coincidentally, or perhaps otherwise, it sort of resembled the body of a rat after ingesting poison. The poor man was hastily buried that same night under the light of lanterns. Elizabeth, now used to widowhood, was very practical about the burial, or was she perhaps hiding something? The slaves were fearful and upset, worried that evil spirits, perhaps in the form of their mistress, had an appetite for death.

In May 1847, a year after Elizabeth lost her fifth husband, Absolom, Elder R. H. Taliaferro of the Enon Baptist Church conducted her sixth marriage ceremony to Willis Routt. It was the third ceremony that the suspicious elder conducted for Elizabeth. Willis Routt apparently, and unfortunately for him, put no stock in the rumors about his new bride.

The final settlement of the estate of Alexander Jeffries, Elizabeth's third husband, did not occur until 1851. Son William received 1/3 and Elizabeth received 2/3 of the final estate, which was her third plus the inheritance of her deceased daughter.

The year 1851 brought sorrow once again to Elizabeth. Her sixth husband Willis died, just three years after their marriage.

Also in 1851, Elizabeth's father, Adam Dale died while living in Elizabeth's fine home in Hazel Green. He was buried at the cemetery near her home where several of her husbands had also been interred. Elizabeth's mother Mary returned to Columbia, Tennessee to live with another daughter.

It is interesting to note that family records name only her last three husbands because of the code of etiquette of the time that three trips to the altar were enough for any respectable and decent woman of high quality.

Neighbor Abner Tate was just one of many who became suspicious of the mysterious deaths of Elizabeth's husbands. Their relationship was precarious at best, for they had had several disagreements over loose livestock ruining cotton crops.

Abner Tate was doing his farm chores one night in 1854 when he was severely wounded by a gunshot. His family assumed that a young neighbor named Billy Saunders had shot him after a disagreement the two men had had earlier in the day. Billy had, on occasion, been called upon to shave Tate. After Tate was shot, Billy was summoned to shave the wounded man, but Tate's family could not detect any sign of guilt in the young man. He showed no discomfort or uneasiness as he performed the task. The family was satisfied that Billy was innocent. Before long, a slave named Jacob, belonging to Elizabeth Routt, was accused of the shooting.

The shooting of Abner Tate had mysterious twists and turns. There was no doubt that the shooting was meant to be fatal. Tate came to the conclusion that his neighbor Elizabeth Routt was behind the shooting.

When the truth finally came out, it appeared that two slaves, Jacob and Fred, committed the shooting. Jacob belonged to Elizabeth Routt, and Fred was owned by Abner Tate.

The reason for the attempt on Tate's life by two slaves was explained in a letter written before Jacob's trial. According to a letter written by Huntsville resident Hugh Lawson Clay to his sister-in-law Virginia dated June 23, 1854, a runaway slave belonging to Mundford

Townsend was staying with Mrs. Routt's slave. "...This negro of Mrs. R[outt] induced him to shoot T[ate], at his mistress' command, who, he declared, said Tate owed her money, which she had sued him for, but could not get as long as he lived. He furnished Townsend's negro with a double-barreled gun belonging to Wm. Jefferies. This is the substance of the admissions of both negroes and there are corroborative circumstances, in great number and of very strong character, confirmatory of their statements in relation to shooting T[ate], while the absence of all motive for the act except the command of Mrs. R[outt], has brought down upon her the prejudices of the people and revived in strength the rumors of her having made way with six husbands. There is no hope of acquitting either negro. I also think Mrs. R[outt] will be obliged to leave the country."

Jacob appeared before the Madison County Circuit Court on Tuesday, March 6, 1855. Jacob was arraigned and charged with murder, for which he pled not guilty. The jury decided otherwise, and found him guilty of murder. They reconvened to assess the dollar value of Jacob, on a motion from Jacob's attorney. After placing a value of $925 on Jacob, Judge Thomas A. Walker ordered that the prisoner be returned to jail and reappear before the court the following Friday to receive his sentence.

Page 123 of the minutes of the Madison County Circuit Court dated Saturday March 10, 1855 recorded that Jacob was brought once again to the bar, and although he was given the chance to speak, he declined to comment. It was ordered that he remain in prison until Friday March 30, at which time he would be hanged in or near Huntsville, between the hours of noon and 2 p.m.

According to a short paragraph in the Wednesday, March 14, 1855 *Southern Advocate,* many people believed that Elizabeth was behind the plot although she was never formally charged. Jacob's accused accomplice was another slave named Fred, who died in jail before he could be brought to trial. D. H. Bingham, a school teacher in Meridianville and Elizabeth Routt's new suitor, stated that Fred gave a statement just before he died that contradicted all his previous confessions. On his death bed, Fred stated, "God knows I had nothing to do with shooting Mr. Tate."

The April 4, 1855 edition of *The Southern Advocate* announced that the execution had been carried out. On Monday April 9, the State of Alabama paid $426.50 to Elizabeth for half the value of Jacob, her executed slave.

Long after Jacob's sentence was carried out, Abner Tate and Elizabeth Routt continued their campaign of slander, slinging accusations in court and other public venues. The culmination of Jacob's trial was only a small subplot in the bizarre story of two people bent on revenge. Bad blood between Elizabeth Routt and her neighbor Abner Tate only got worse.

Now at age 60, Elizabeth persuaded her new suitor D.H. Bingham, to accuse Abner Tate of murder, concocting a bizarre story that resulted in a sensational trial. Tate was tried for murdering a man 16 years earlier, and it was suggested that he had murdered a second man. His trial began the last day of December 1855 and finished on Friday, January 4, 1856. He was found innocent

After the trial, Abner Tate paid Huntsville novelist (and cousin to Mark Twain) Jeremiah Clemens to write a salacious pamphlet against Elizabeth Routt and D. H. Bingham. Tate acknowledged that he paid $500.00 to Clemens to write the 56 page document. It was Tate's own public defense against the slanderous accusations by Elizabeth Routt and D. H. Bingham.

Not long after the completion of the booklet, the following story was printed in *The Selma Sentinel*:

"We have received a pamphlet of some sixty pages from Abner Tate of Huntsville, Alabama, being a defense of himself against the charge of a double murder, committed by him several years ago, which charges were preferred by on D.H. Bingham. Mr. Tate, when these charges were preferred, was arrested and investigation had before the Mayor of Huntsville and two Magistrates."

"There was no evidence adduced going to show the guilt of Mr. Tate, and consequently he was discharged. The pamphlet contains many strange things and altogether, it is the most strange case we have ever heard of, one in which great mystery is certainly involved."

The booklet written by Jeremiah Clemens was filled with venom and spite. One excerpt claimed that around Elizabeth's marriage bed, "six grinning skeletons were already hung." It went on to say "...poor soul she is alone - she ought to have a husband. And then such a husband - an industrious sober husband like D.H. Bingham. She has not been particularly fortunate in that respect heretofore, and in Bingham's opinion was entitled to all the consolation an industrious sober man can bring to the bed around which nightly assembles a conclave of ghosts to witness the endearments that once were theirs and shudder through their fleshless forms at the fiendish spirit which wraps the grave worm in the bridal garment and infused a lingering death with a conjugal kiss. The worst fate I could wish for Bingham would be the success of his undertaking, but I doubt whether the prize will ever be his. He is dealing with a shrewd bad woman and she may calculate that she can induce him to goad me beyond endurance. The clasps of her arm around his neck would call up dreadful shapes to sit upon his dreaming pillow and make his nights as fearful."

"Mr. Bingham has failed but he deserves the possession of the venerable bride and I trust that happiness will not be denied him. The union is one so eminently fit and proper that it would be a pity to prevent its accomplishment. There is no crime, no vice, no detestable meanness that is not familiar to one or both of them and though the dead should flee away in shuddering horror from the bridal chamber there will be enough of grinning friends to witness the ceremony and congratulate the happy pair."

Jere Clemens wrote the following poem about Elizabeth:

"As if the dead could feel
The icy worm around them steal
and shudder as the reptiles creep
To revel o'er their rotting sleep."

Bingham was livid and not about to let the accusations against him go unanswered. An excerpt written to *The Athens Herald* states:

"It is known that he (Tate) is illiterate and scarcely able to put together three consecutive lines in the English language; while the pamphlet exhibits in its arrangement and details professional skill and tact.

It is written by the one (Clemens) to whom rumor attributes it, he is a man of intellect, genius, and talent; naturally towering, lofty and noble, capable of wielding the scepter of an Empire, mentally; and were his mental qualifications backed and sustained by a moral courage and integrity of purpose, sufficient to resist those inebriating excitant that debase his lofty genius and bring it down to the groveling level of those who bow and cringe for hire, at the shrine of mannon, he would be morally worthy of wearing the proudest diadem within the gift of the enlightened people of this fair Republic."

Bingham continued with his explanation: "Having succeeded in obtaining an acquittal, they were not satisfied in letting the matter rest, but in the excess of their joy, made a publication in which the facts of the case were grossly perverted, falsified and misrepresented the character of witness and prosecutor of witness and prosecutor grossly vilified."

Still, there was the matter of Elizabeth's serial widowhood. She had already gained the attention of a number of people for the sudden and mysterious deaths of her many husbands and the church had withdrawn her membership. Abner Tate blatantly accused her of murdering her husbands.

A complaint was filed on August 9, 1856. Elizabeth E. Routt sued Abner Tate for $50,000 for the publication of his pamphlet called "Defense of Abner Tate against Charges of Murder Preferred by D.A. Bingham."

But the trial would never take place. The suit was dismissed because Elizabeth had already moved to Marshall County, Mississippi and sold her plantation to Levi Donaldson for $12,500. Defendant Abner Tate asked that the court dismiss the charges and that he recover any costs incurred by him from Mrs. Routt. The court agreed to consider the motion.

In 1860, Abner Tate moved to south Alabama, just before the outbreak of the Civil War. As far as history books are concerned, the mystery of the missing men he was accused of killing has never been explained.

After Elizabeth's mother died in 1865, Elizabeth's sister, Mrs. Vaught, had their father's body moved to Rose Hill Cemetery in Columbia, Tennessee. Elizabeth Routt died on May 7, 1866 in Marshall County, Mississippi.

Epilogue

The official Alabama Guide Book says that Elizabeth was a fascinating lady of many marriages. Folklore says that she had a hat rack near her door that displayed one hat from each of her dead husbands.

Elizabeth had the body of her first husband removed from Centerville, Tennessee and taken to Columbia. His interesting tombstone is in the shape of a pulpit with an open Bible on top.

Elizabeth Dale Gibbons Flanagan
Jeffries High Brown Routt

The personal feud of two people, supposedly started by loose livestock, destroyed reputations and fortunes, and caused the deaths of two slaves. All that remains of the mystery today is found in the pages of court records, the ruins of the plantation home destroyed by arson in 1968, and a small, crowded graveyard under an immense holly tree a mile east of Hazel Green. The steps and remnants of three fireplaces are all that are left of the home of the mysterious Elizabeth Routt, who took the truth with her when she died.

Although Elizabeth is thought to be buried in Mississippi, there are those who believe her ghost still haunts the home she knew for many years. Thick holly trees hide the site from casual passersby, but on clear nights when the stars are bright, some say they see lanterns through the trees. Could it be Elizabeth burying one of her husbands in secrecy? While most people accept that explanation, there are others who believe she is searching for her next husband. Were Elizabeth's husbands murdered, or the victims of bad luck? It must have been bad luck, for it was never proven otherwise.

The Bell Witch

If you are faint of heart or afraid of things that go bump in the night, then read no further. However, if the prospect of an encounter with a disembodied voice or a shadowy figure doesn't frighten you, then proceed... with caution.

The following is the true story of a haunting that began nearly 200 years ago. Eyewitnesses and family members long ago recorded chilling accounts of their experience with the entity that became known world-wide as the Bell Witch.

In 1817, 68-year-old John Bell, his wife Lucy, and their seven children, lived in the Robertson County town of Red River, Tennessee, situated 12 miles north of Springfield. John Bell needed to be a respected pillar of his community, but his pride and his secrets were his undoing. His life began to unravel when he made an enemy of his neighbor, Kate Batts, a corpulent 40ish woman who lived on the next farm. John offered to buy property from Kate and her husband, who had become an invalid in an accident. As a neighborly gesture, John offered to sell them one of his slaves to help on the Batts farm, as well as a loan of cash. Because the rate of interest was not specified at the beginning of the transaction, Kate Batts was furious when she discovered how much interest he wanted on the loan. According to those who were there to hear it, she cast a spell on John Bell and his family:

"...let me offer you a witch's malefaction, Old John Bell: you may have your broad acres...your big house and your salubricated health right now. But just wait and see what sad changes shall soon descend upon you. And more than you among the Bells."

Kate Batts sued him in court. Bell lost the suit, and the other elders in the Red River Baptist Church felt they had no other choice but to ex-communicate him. To John Bell, losing his status in the church, and thus the community, was the biggest disgrace of all.

In the early fall of 1817, John Bell encountered a huge animal that looked like nothing he had ever seen before. It's eyes glowered at him from the edge of the cornfield. He raised his rifle and aimed it at the creature. His aim was true, he fired, but instead of falling to the ground, the creature disappeared without a trace.

Over the next few weeks, other visions appeared to Bell and his family.

Soon, there were strange noises in the still of the night. The family was awakened night after night by knocking on the outside walls, doors, and shutters. When Bell got up to investigate, the noises stopped, but commenced again when everyone was settled back into bed. The children were barely able to stay awake in school.

The entity seemed to evolve, becoming stronger, louder, and more frightening. Everyone in the family except for John's wife Lucy, began to experience pains similar to pin pricks. They were awakened by the sound of rats scurrying in the room and gnawing on their bedposts. When they got up to search for the source of the noise, they found nothing. Soon they heard the sound of someone smacking their lips very loudly. Those sounds were followed with disgusting gagging, strangling, and vomiting noises, the sound of fighting dogs, and heavy chains being drug across the floor.

John Bell's tongue would swell, filling his entire mouth. He had difficulty eating and swallowing. As the entity evolved, it acquired a voice. At first, the frightened family heard whispers, then raucous laughter, and finally she began to speak in a clear voice. John Bell warned his family not to tell anyone in the community. They were suffering, but it was only the beginning. The entity that would become known as the Bell Witch, ominously warned that she would not end her terror until one member of the family was dead. And she kept her promise.

The spectre that haunted John Bell

Throughout the year 1818, the Bell Witch vented her anger at the helpless family. The innocent children could not understand why they were attacked. In the middle of the night, the witch would rip covers off of the frightened victims as they slept, tear the ticking from the beds, and pull feathers out of the mattresses. It laughed hideously and panted loudly. The two family members who suffered the most were John Bell and his pretty 12-year-old daughter, Betsy. John Bell's face would contort, and he was struck repeatedly by unseen hands. Betsy's hair was pulled and twisted, and she was drug out of her bed by her hair. She was slapped so hard that red marks would appear on her face. Even when she slept at the homes of her friends, the witch attacked her.

John Bell could no longer keep the secret within the walls of his home. He did not want to become a curiosity in the community and be accused of being a fraud, but he was desperate for help. He told his closest, most trusted friends, who came to witness for themselves. Among his friends was a minister who came to quote scriptures in an attempt to drive the demon away. The witch listened, but seemed to be amused by the man she would forevermore refer to as "Old Sugar Mouth."

Visitors to the Bell household experienced the frightening manifestations as the spirit grew stronger.

Word of the strange happenings spread throughout the community, and remembering the ominous threat by Kate Batts, some dubbed it, "Kate Batts' Witch." Kate was shunned and lost her friends. Others referred to it as "The Bell Witch."

The Bell Witch soon entertained the many people who gathered night after night in the parlor of the Bell home to witness the curiosity. She enjoyed tattling on the neighbors who failed to attend Sunday's church services and other infractions. People who told lies or stole from others, smug in the belief that they had gotten away with something, would soon be ratted out to guests in the Bell home. Attendance at church suddenly improved and there was a new-found sense of honesty among those who ran fast and loose with the truth.

The witch's malevolence to John Bell, referred by her as "Old Jack," was pure and especially heinous. Her loathsome treatment of Betsy was curiously mixed with occasional tenderness and concern. On the other hand, she loved Lucy Bell, or "Old Luce" as she affectionately called her. When asked to explain her contradictory behavior, she said that Old Luce was pure and good, while Old Jack was evil, even though she would not reveal why. It was evident to everyone however, that as the attacks on Betsy decreased, John's suffering increased.

As word of the Bell Witch spread, visitors soon came from all over the world. Even though they stayed at the Bell household and ate their food, John Bell never charged for their room and board, making sure he could not be accused of gleaning a profit from the phenomena. One of their visitors had been a fellow soldier with John Bell, Jr., none other than General Andrew Jackson.

General Jackson made his way to the Bell home with an entourage of curious men, and a wagon containing tents and provisions, in anticipation of spending several nights camped outside the home. As they approached the Bell home, two men openly discussed the witch and their belief that it was a hoax. Suddenly the wagon stopped. No matter how much they coaxed and prodded, the horses could not budge the wagon free from the unknown and unseen restraints. General Jackson dismounted his horse and thoroughly inspected the wagon, finding nothing physically wrong with it. He stood up and chuckled, "What else could it be but the Bell's witch?" The witch whispered some words to General Jackson, and the wagon was suddenly freed.

When they arrived at the Bell farm, Jackson introduced a member of his group who claimed to be a witch chaser. After eating supper, everyone went into the parlor to talk. The man who claimed to have the power to remove the witch began to taunt her and pulled out a pistol with a silver bullet in the chamber. The others listened in disbelief to his ridiculous bragging for some time. When he at last ran out of wonderful things to say about himself, a silence fell over the room.

Faint footsteps could be heard in the distance, then became increasingly louder until it sounded like a large man stomping his feet. A disembodied voice announced to General Jackson that she was ready for business. The witch commenced to make a fool out of the witch chaser. She asked the man what he was waiting for, and told him she was directly in front of him. Twice he pulled the trigger, and twice the pistol failed to shoot. She then announced that it was her turn. The frightened man was hauled up to his tiptoes as if someone had their fingers inside his nostrils, pulling upward. He was repeatedly slapped and thrown to the floor. He screamed in pain as he was again hauled up to his tiptoes by his nostrils. The door opened by itself and the man was led outside by his nose, stumbling the whole way. He ran to the road and was not seen again. Most agreed he deserved it.

General Jackson was greatly amused, and laughed at the spectacle, but the witch announced to General Jackson that she would return the following night to expose another of his party as a fraud. Jackson and his men spent the night encamped outside the house, but the next morning, several members of his party convinced Jackson that they needed to get on the road, no doubt afraid that they might be the object of that evening's entertainment. With that, they left the Bell farm.

Although the witch mistreated Betsy, she could also be benevolent and protective of her. One day in May, 1820, Betsy Bell and two of her friends decided to take a horseback ride. The spirit warned them not to go; a terrible storm was coming from the north. They ignored her advice, and rode northwest until they came to a river that was still quite swollen from recent heavy rains. They sat on their horses in a copse of poplar trees when the wind suddenly picked up and caused the trees to sway. One of the teens said that they would be better off to stay in the trees for shelter when the spirit cried out to them to get to the other side of the river or they would be crushed by the trees that would soon be uprooted by the strong winds. Again, they did not heed the spirit's instructions, and tried to run in the direction of the Bell farm. The horses refused to go. The spirit called out for them to cross the river, even though they were afraid they would drown in the deep water, now rolling in waves from the high winds. In an angry voice, the spirit ordered them to hold on to the reins and say nothing to the horses. This time, they did as they were told, and the horses carried them to safety on the other side. They watched as many of the poplars they planned to use as shelter were toppled in the storm.

Betsy was once again among a group of friends that went to explore in the nearby cave the Bells used to keep their food cold. It was June, 1820, and the young people wanted to eat their lunch inside the cool cave. A nine-year-old boy was crawling through a passageway when part of it collapsed around the top half of his body. He cried out for help, but the others could not tell which direction his voice was coming from. Then his candle went out. He called out, but his voice was so faint. Betsy asked the others to be quiet, because she could not hear him. Suddenly the voice of the witch said, "That's because he's buried."

A glow of light appeared in the passageway and led to where the helpless boy was trapped. He was grabbed by his ankles by unseen hands that pulled him from the muck, saving his life.

The Bell Witch was ever-present when the family was assembled, and once when Lucy asked if anyone in the family had heard whether or not her son Jesse had arrived from a long journey to his home less than a mile away, the witch told Lucy that she would go check for her. She reported back that he was safely at home, writing by candlelight at the table. When asked the next day, Jesse said that while he was writing, there was a knock at the front door. It opened by itself, then quickly closed by itself.

In September 1820, Lucy became gravely ill with pleurisy. Her condition worsened over the next few weeks, and the witch kept a constant vigil at her bedside, along with her family. The witch sang Lucy's favorite hymns in a most beautiful voice and cried out, "Poor Luce, poor Luce!" Every morning when she awoke, the witch asked Lucy how she was feeling. As Lucy's condition got progressively worse, the witch begged her in a very sorrowful voice to eat in order to keep up her strength. But Lucy was too sick to eat the delicious meals brought by caring neighbors. Knowing that Lucy especially loved grapes and hazelnuts, the witch instructed her to hold her hands open one day. Out of nowhere, nuts, and then grapes fell out of thin air into her outstretched hands. The witch even cracked the nuts open so she could eat them. She prattled on in conversation until Lucy would say she was too tired to talk anymore. The witch would become silent until Lucy was next awake. John Bell kept away from his wife's bedside because the witch continued to berate him, and he was adamant that Lucy be able to rest in peace. No one was more joyful than the strange entity when Lucy finally recovered.

The Bell Witch delighted in pulling pranks. She would manifest herself as a nimble rabbit when the men took their hounds out to hunt, causing the dogs to collapse in exhaustion after failing to catch the prize. She repeated the story many times to visitors, laughing at her own cleverness. She once told her audience that she was the spirit of a pioneer who had hidden a large amount of gold and was then killed by hostile Indians. She told the men where the gold was buried, instructed only certain men to dig for it, and made them promise to give the fortune to Betsy. They dug and dug, but found nothing. The witch laughed for weeks about how she had fooled them.

John Bell's health was rapidly deteriorating by the fall of 1820, brought on by the attacks against him. The witch announced that he would be dead by Christmas, and her verbal and physical attacks on him increased. On October 28th, he left the house for the last time. While walking out to the hog pens with his son Richard, one of his shoes suddenly flew off his foot and was hurled some distance away. His son retrieved the shoe and put it back on his father's foot, tying the knot extra securely. After a few steps, the other shoe flew off in the same manner. Once again, the young boy retrieved and replaced his father's shoe. John finished his task at the hog pens, then the two started back to the home. Suddenly, John fell to the ground as if his feet had been yanked from under him. His shoes were forcefully pulled from his feet and flung in different directions by the unseen force. John's face was being beaten and pummeled by the force and he was in obvious pain. Then the spirit began to sing loudly and finally left with an Indian war cry. John went into the home and took to his bed.

Throughout the next few weeks, the witch taunted John constantly. On the morning of December 19, 1820, John was still sound asleep when Lucy woke up. It was very unusual since he was always the first of the family to get up. After completing the daily chores, Lucy went to check on John, only to find that he appeared to be in a coma. When John, Jr. checked the medicine chest, he discovered a strange bottle with a black liquid in it. No one had seen it before. The doctor was summoned, and some of the neighbors waited by John's bedside. With everyone assembled, the witch announced that she had gotten Old Jack and "...he was a goner...." She also acknowledged that she had poisoned John in his sleep and gave a hideous laugh. The doctor said that he believed the poison to be an extract of nightshade berry, and there was nothing left for him to do.

Friends, neighbors, and family took up a death watch throughout the night. Occasionally the Bell Witch would return to sing some bawdy song and ask if he was still alive. On the morning of Wednesday, December 20, John Bell took his last breath.

His funeral was held inside the home because he had been excommunicated from the church. Many people attended, and he was buried in the family cemetery near the home. As the last clods of dirt were thrown over his coffin, the Bell Witch could be heard singing "Row Me Up Some Brandy, Oh" as if she were in a drunken stupor. She continued to sing as the mourners walked back into the house.

That night, a heavy snow fell around the Bell home. The witch returned to converse with the family, but only John, Jr. would speak to her. He was angry and demanded to know what her reason was, now that she had succeeded in causing his father's death. She refused an explanation, but they got into a long discussion about life and death. John, Jr. said he could not believe anything the witch said anyway, and that he would not be fooled. She told him to go to the window so she could show him proof that she could fool him when she wanted. As he watched, faraway footprints appeared in the snow, as if someone was walking to the house. She told John, Jr. to get his father's boots and compare them to the footprints. He already knew they were an exact match.

During one of her visits, the witch foretold major events for the future of America. The shackles of slavery would be removed from the Negro race as a result of a terrible war between Americans. America would be involved in another war that would involve many nations, and again many Americans would die. After this war, America would emerge as the most powerful nation on earth, but much poverty would affect America in an economic depression. Twenty years after the first major war, another world-wide war, much more devastating than the first, would kill even more people and cause more destruction.

In the few weeks after John Bell's death, visitations from the Bell Witch became fewer and farther in between. She had accomplished her goal, but she still had one more task to tend to - she needed to ensure the happiness of young Betsy Bell.

Betsy was now 15-years-old and rumors in the community were that she was about to marry Joshua Gardner. The Bell Witch was adamantly opposed. She made her strenuous objections known to the couple, and then pleaded with Betsy's brother John to prevent the union. The only reason she gave was to say that Betsy would never know one day of happiness for the rest of her life. Although Betsy and Joshua were formally engaged, Betsy was worn down by the witch until she called off the wedding. The witch was now finished with the Bell family.

The Bell Witch made her exit one day while the family was assembled near the fireplace. A ball of smoke rolled out of the chimney and hovered near the hearth. The voice of the Bell Witch told the family that they were free of her. The ball dissolved into smoke and rose back into the chimney.

In 1824, Betsy married Richard Powell, the kind man who had been her school teacher during her youth. Betsy Bell was finally happy.

Many books and stories have been written about the Bell Witch. Two stand out in particular, "The Bell

Witch of Tennessee," written by Dr. Charles Bailey Bell, son of John Bell, Jr. in 1934, and "The Bell Witch, An American Haunting," written by Brent Monahan in 1997.

The unusual circumstances surrounding Brent Monahan's book make it particularly interesting. Richard Powell, the man who married Betsy Bell, knew the family quite well during the period of the haunting by the Bell Witch. Shortly before his death, he wrote an account of the haunting and the aftermath, for his young daughter to read only in the event of the return of the Bell Witch. It was sealed in an envelope and never opened by her.

Richard Powell's accounts are verified by other writings on the subject, including Dr. Charles Bell's book. What it offers however, is a description of the final encounter with the Bell Witch, and finally the reason for the haunting, which he discovered several years after his marriage to Betsy.

One evening, Powell was having trouble sleeping, and rather than keep his wife awake with his tossing and turning, he got up to sleep in the guest room. As he made his way down the hall, he heard a sound of rocks tossed on the roof. Afraid that the noises would upset his wife, he went back to their bed. The next night, he again got up after having trouble falling asleep, and this time he heard the sound of cats fighting, rocks on the windows, and a sound similar to a bobcat walking on the roof. He returned to bed, but began to wonder if it was the warning of the return of the Bell Witch.

Suspecting that it was more strongly tied to Betsy herself, he read about a version of hypnotism and decided to try it out on Betsy. Betsy fell into a trance and answered a few superficial questions. When the questions became more focused on the events of the previous nights, the voice of the Bell Witch returned to answer them herself. Richard Powell was able to ascertain the reason for the original haunting.

When Betsy was 12-years-old, she was an attractive and happy young lady. Her father began to mistreat her however, and the strange noises were warnings to John Bell to stay away from Betsy. Though it was now obvious why the witch wanted to kill John Bell, it still wasn't apparent why Betsy was attacked so viciously. The witch explained that she was angry at Betsy for not telling anyone about her father. The witch was instrumental in Bell's death by poisoning him with nightshade, but she would not leave until she caused Betsy to break off her engagement with Joshua Gardner, insisting that she would never know a day of happiness if she married him.

The reason for the return of the Bell Witch after so

many years was even more disturbing to Richard Powell. She explained that she had come back to protect Betsy's daughter from her husband. Powell was dumbfounded and horrified by the insinuation. He promised that his daughter would always be protected by him, and the Bell Witch once again vanished.

After Powell's death in 1842, Betsy and her daughter moved to Panola County, Mississippi. The manuscript was discovered in the attic of a distant relative of Richard Powell's in January, 1995. Over 150 years after his death, his story was finally published.

The Bell Witch promised to return in 1935 to visit another member of the Bell family, though no one knows if it came to pass. There are those who staunchly believe that she still haunts the area where the Bell home once stood. The story of the Bell Witch still fascinates and draws visitors to the Tennessee site. You too may wish to visit the witch's haunt, however, if you harbor a liar's tongue or a dishonest disposition, perhaps you would be wise to by-pass the site of the Bell home as you pass near Adams, Tennessee. Otherwise, you may feel the not-so-imaginary prick of a thousand pins.

The Ghost of Brown's Ferry Road

A cedar stake once marked the spot where John T. White was brutally murdered. The ground around the stake was barren, as if the vegetation had been poisoned. Perhaps it was the blood shed on this very spot which kept the spot naked. The sadness, horror, and shattered dreams seeped into the soil along with the ebbing life of a young man who had, only moments before his death, looked forward to the happiest day of his life.

John T. White stood on the raft crossing Brown's Ferry in North Alabama and looked at the opposite shore. As he gazed across the wide Tennessee River, his thoughts were of his future bride in Virginia. He was on his way to meet his betrothed and looked forward to the impending wedding and the long and happy life with the woman he loved. The year was 1840, and it would be a long journey indeed.

White was traveling with two footmen. They left Brown's Ferry Landing early that morning, and White stopped to enjoy breakfast with Colonel Bartley Cox, who had a tavern near the ferry and was well known for his hospitality and good food. White's footmen walked on without him with the intention of meeting up later that morning.

After a pleasant visit and breakfast, John, in a good mood, resumed his walk toward Athens, Alabama. The sun was rising in the morning sky, and he was anxious to get to his journey once again. Along the way, he encountered two brothers who identified themselves as the Thorntons. The brothers greeted John and commented on the weather before bidding farewell and going about in opposite directions.

After passing John, the brothers exchanged glances and looked warily around to make sure there was no one else on the path coming in either direction. Perhaps in their brief conversation with John White, they realized that he was traveling virtually alone and found him to be an easy mark. One or both of the Thorntons turned and fired at the stranger. The bullet met its mark and the stranger, who had so much to look forward to in his young life, was now dead.

Swiftly, the killers dragged his body off the path

and went through White's pockets. They were disappointed in the amount of cash he was carrying, however in their haste they missed five hundred dollars which had been sewn in the waistband of his underclothes. They left his body and ran.

John White's body was discovered later by another traveler and carried into the nearest town of Athens. A grave was dug in the old Athens City Cemetery and he was buried, among strangers. His betrothed would never see him again.

Though much information has been lost to the abyss of time, it is apparent that the identity of the killers was somehow discovered, perhaps by a witness to the murder, and a posse was formed to apprehend the killers.

Hiram Higgins, a 38-year-old leader in the community, volunteered to be in charge of the posse. Higgins was a distinguished architect and had designed the Limestone County Courthouse which was completed five years before the murder of John White.

The posse followed the killers north. They were on the trail in Nashville and apprehended one of the men at "the old bridge" just as he got across. The posse was diligent and would not be satisfied with the capture of only one of the men. The thunderous hooves of their horses continued north over the Kentucky state line. Within a short time, they captured the other half of the murderous thieves at Franklin, Kentucky. They were brought to Limestone County to face justice for their crimes.

Although John White was unknown to the people of Alabama, his murder would not go unpunished. The Thornton brothers were members of the community, but there was no justification for what they had done.

The first brother was brought to trial in Athens, Alabama. He was found guilty of murder and he was swiftly executed. Mark Thornton was charged and arraigned in Limestone County as well, and pleaded not guilty. His attorney filed a motion to have the trial moved because of the overwhelming amount of publicity. His attorney argued that a jury of twelve men who had not heard about the case could not be impaneled in Limestone County. The change of venue was granted and his trial was moved to nearby Huntsville, in Madison County.

On October 29, 1840, Mark Thornton appeared before Judge George Washington Lane in the Madison County Circuit Court on a motion to have the trial date set. Attorney William Acklin prosecuted for the State of Alabama. Thirty-six jurors were summoned and twelve were chosen to sit in judgment of the defendant.

The trial began on November 3 in the Madison County Courthouse. The defendant pleaded not guilty and the jury heard a portion of the evidence in the case.

At the close of the day, the judge called for a recess until the following morning. The attorneys agreed to allow the jurors to go to their respective homes for the evening. Mark Thornton was returned to his jail cell.

The next morning, the jury returned for the remainder of testimony and closing arguments from both attorneys. The judge gave the jury instructions and they left to decide the fate of Mark Thornton.

After some time, the jury returned. When asked by the judge, the foreman read the decision of the jury. "We the jury find the defendant guilty as charged in the indictment." The jury then recommended mercy for Thornton.

Sheriff William Robinson escorted Mark Thornton before Judge Lane on November 11 for sentencing. When asked by Judge Lane if he knew of any reason why the sentence of the court should not be passed on him, Mark Thornton was silent.

The judge announced his decision in the case of John White's robbery and senseless murder. "The court then orders that, you, Mark Thornton, be carried back to the jail from whence you came, and you there be kept in close confinement until the eleventh day of December next, and on that day, between the hours of ten o'clock a.m. and four o'clock p.m. you be taken from there to the place of execution, and be there hung by the neck until dead."

On December 11, Mark Thornton was taken from his jail cell and escorted to the hanging tree two blocks from the courthouse. His knees must have buckled as he took his final steps on that cold day.

For many years after the death of John White, the cedar stake remained on the spot where he was killed. Many people believed that the killing place was haunted and no vegetation grew in that area. Strange sounds were heard by passersby and many claimed to see misshapen shadows. Some saw the struggling helpless victim who was doomed to an early death, while others claimed to have seen the dark images of evil that had, years before, consumed the innocent traveler. Anyone who was brave enough to pass the spot after dark took a lantern or a shotgun. Even the most courageous whistled as they passed the cedar stake. Still, no amount of clothing could mask the unmistakable chill in the air that raised the hackles of travelers passing over the barren ground.

More than a century and a half have passed since the murder of John T. White. His grave in the old Athens Cemetery is unmarked, and perhaps never was. The location of the graves of his killers are unknown as well. The cedar stake that once marked where John White took his final breath on earth is also gone and lost to time. Perhaps the spirits of evil have moved on and John White can finally rest in peace.

The Era of Violence

The year 1916 was a landmark year in Huntsville, Alabama's history. Judge W. Thomas Lawler had just been re-elected as Probate Judge in an election filled with mud-slinging, blackmail, and accusations of corruption. On Wednesday, June 14, he failed to meet his wife at the evening Chatauqua. His glasses were found on the street near the courthouse next to his abandoned car. Everyone feared the worst for the 52-year-old judge.

On Saturday June 17, Sheriff Robert Phillips watched from the iron bridge at Whitesburg as volunteers pulled a body out of the murky waters of the Tennessee River. One of the excited men wiped mud from the face of the human remains and confirmed what they already suspected. The judge was no longer a missing person.

Lawler's pockets had been filled with metal weights and an iron weight had been tied to his waist. There was a bullet hole in his chest.

The townspeople were shocked at the murder and rumors flew like a Wild West wind. David Overton, one of the men who ran against Lawler in the recent election, was nowhere to be found. He was an instant and obvious suspect. Bad blood between the two men was known far and wide and both men had tried to undermine the other in order to get elected. Lawler even went so far as to have illegal moonshine planted in Overton's barn.

Shelby Pleasant's Home

Judge Lawler's funeral service was held at the First Methodist Church on Greene Street. The auditorium seated 200 people, and twice that number stood outside the church to show their respect and perhaps glean a little gossip. His funeral at Maple Hill Cemetery was the largest ever held in the historic graveyard.

Meanwhile, David Overton was still missing. He had served as the Chief of Police for 12 years, worked as the dispenser for Madison County until prohibition went into effect, and was elected clerk of the circuit in Madison County. He had appeared to be a model citizen until charges were brought against him for buying votes. It seems that then, just as now, getting elected, no matter what means, was a big deal. To make matters worse, he was accused of bribing Madison County Circuit Solicitor (District Attorney) Zack Drake to influence the grand jury in his favor.

His trial began in November 1913. His defense attorneys were Shelby Pleasants and Robert Spragins. A mistrial was declared when the male jurors could not reach a unanimous verdict and the trial was rescheduled for the following February. By then, two witnesses had vanished, the charges were dropped, and Overton went back to work.

Judge Lawler was having problems of his own at that time. Impeachment proceedings were brought against him for missing money, but when the money was accounted for, charges were dropped.

In May 1916, Judge Lawler, David Overton, and Zack Drake all wanted to be elected as Circuit Judge.

It appeared to be a close race between Overton and Lawler, and when the votes had been counted, Lawler had beat Overton by just over 300 votes. Drake went to the Law and Equity Court and complained that the election had violated the Corrupt Practice Act, and an investigation ensued.

A grand jury was convened to look into evidence that the two men had illegally solicited votes by offering money. If found guilty, their careers would be gone and they would face time in jail. They were both desperate men.

All of that took a back seat when Judge Lawler was murdered. Rumors of a conspiracy circulated, and a number of men were considered suspects. Still, the townspeople felt that the key to the murder was held by the missing David Overton, and they waited.

Attorney Shelby Pleasants, one of the two attorneys who had represented David Overton in the 1913 trial, was acting strangely. He was a nervous and sensitive man, but well-respected. The 42-year-old man had once served as Madison County Circuit Solicitor. He had never married, and lived in a Victorian home on Walker Avenue. As an attorney, and especially as a Circuit Solicitor, he abhorred controversy and confrontation. But something happened, and he couldn't take any more.

On Wednesday, June 21, just two weeks after Judge

Lawler was reported as missing, Shelby Pleasants said good-bye to his secretary Katie Sanford, as she left the office for a late lunch. Pleasants took out a sheet of paper and hurriedly wrote something on it. He closed the door of his office and shot himself in the head. His secretary became hysterical when she discovered his body on the floor next to his overturned chair. The revolver was still in his hand and a bullet wound was over his right ear.

The note he left explained that the murder investigation was too much of a strain for him and he insisted that he was in no way involved in the murder of Judge Lawler. He was afraid that because he had represented Overton at one time, he would be somehow implicated. He too was buried at Maple Hill Cemetery, but the incident would not be forgotten.

Two days later, another drama rocked the stunned townspeople. Sheriff Robert Phillips shot himself to death in his office. His suicide note, though somewhat cryptic, implied that he had been part of the conspiracy. Like the two men before him, Sheriff Phillips was buried at Maple Hill Cemetery.

Two months after Judge Lawler's death, David Overton was captured in Tennessee. He told the story of the night Lawler died, and confirmed that he had fired the fatal shot. He said it was an act of self-defense, and although his story appeared genuine, the fact that he ran from the scene may have ultimately condemned him. He was found guilty and sentenced to death. At the train depot on Church Street, David Overton climbed on board the 10:40 train bound for Birmingham, a physically and emotionally sick man. In March, 1917, Overton was killed in an elaborately arranged escape attempt. Amid rumors that his death was also arranged, David Overton's body was brought to Huntsville and buried, where else, Maple Hill Cemetery.

Nearly 100 years later, scholars and historians still discuss and argue the details of this most interesting case. Some feel that Overton should have been acquitted of the death. Although he may have had thoughts of turning himself in, some believe that it was Sheriff Phillips who arranged for his escape as well as the disappearance of Judge Lawler's body. The suicide of Shelby Pleasants remains a mystery as well, and a later resident of his home believes that he still walks the halls.

It appears that no expense was spared in the construction of the lavender Victorian home on Walker Avenue. Glazed tiles with Indian motifs decorate the fireplaces and an old world ambiance speaks of class and culture. A long time owner of the house has a different view of the home. Many years ago, he got up one night to walk down the hall to the bathroom. In the darkness, he saw the shadow of his grown son Jack, and stumbled into him as they passed each other. They did not speak though, and something rather odd about his countenance stayed with him. The next morning, over breakfast, the owner remarked to his wife about the event and remarked that Jack smelled like blood and asked what she could make out of the situation. "Jack isn't here," she said. "He's out of town."

The owner of the house was very much disturbed, knowing he had encountered a ghost. He shivered as a chill shot down his spine and the hair on his neck stood up. Although he never encountered the ghost of Shelby Pleasants again, he frequently heard the sound of a woman crying softly and a man's voice trying to comfort her. Could it have been the mournful cries of Shelby Pleasants' mother wishing for her son to return? Perhaps Shelby's voice is heard trying to soothe his heartbroken mother.

Many unanswered questions remain regarding the incidents surrounding Judge Lawler's death. No one will ever know the reason Shelby Pleasants took his own life, and no connection to the crime has ever surfaced. Today the pretty Victorian house is the home of a young family. The laughter of children fills the home, and perhaps Shelby Pleasants has finally found the peace he desperately needed.

Rev. Robert Donnell

Restless Spirits of the Donnell House

Sometime in the late 1840s, the Reverend Robert Donnell and his second wife, Clara Lindley Donnell, began work on their new house, a two-story wood frame plantation home in Athens, Alabama. It was not an especially grand house, compared to those of the wealthy in that period of time, but it was comfortable and welcoming. "Pleasant Hill" had two formal parlors, a dining room, a detached kitchen, three bedrooms upstairs, and slave quarters. Columns held up the two-story porch and a long walkway led to the wide front door.

Reverend Donnell, known locally as Father Donnell, had come from pioneer stock, Scots-Irish roots, and a strictly religious upbringing. He read the Bible several times in his youth and wanted to be a minister, despite his lack of formal education. An education was out of the question for the young man. His father had been in the American Revolution and fought at Guilford County Courthouse in North Carolina. When the family left to migrate south, his father died shortly after they arrived in Wilson County, Tennessee. At age 15, Robert became the sole support of the family.

In 1810, a schism occurred in the Presbyterian Church, and a new denomination was formed. The Cumberland Presbyterian Church did not require ministers to have a formal education, and Robert Donnell found an answer to his prayers. He and his cousin, Robert Bell, became ministers in the newly-formed congregation, and rode all over the Mississippi Territory to spread the Gospel. They founded many churches, and were among those Cumberland Presbyterian ministers described as "flaming fires" for their enthusiasm.

Reverend Robert Donnell met his future wife while conducting a camp meeting in Tennessee. Ann Eliza Smith was the daughter of a wealthy man, and the two married in 1818. After only 10 years of marriage, the frail Mrs. Donnell died, following four of their five children to the grave. James Webb Smith Donnell, the couple's only surviving son, was left without a mother at the tender age of eight.

A few years later, Reverend Donnell married Clarissa Lindley, a native of Ohio. She was a good mother to his son, and well-loved by everyone who knew her. When J.W.S. Donnell married a Greenbrier girl, "Mother Donnell" was a good mother-in-law and grandmother to their many children.

Father Donnell decided to settle down in Athens. He felt that he was good at planting churches, but he would not leave because the slaves he had inherited from the estate of his first wife had relatives on nearby plantations. Donnell was torn by the issue of slavery, and at that time, it was illegal in Alabama to live as a freed slave. Therefore, if he had set his slaves free, they would be forced to leave their families anyway. He was concerned about their spiritual welfare, and insisted that they come in every day to the dining room of his home, where they began their day in prayers.

In 1853, Reverend Donnell became ill during a camp meeting. His illness worsened, and in 1855, the feeble giant of a man died in his home. His wife moved into a small home and J.W.S. Donnell and his children moved into the plantation home.

J.W.S. "Jim" Donnell had a good head for business. His wealth multiplied and he was a well-known man in the community. He sold wood to the Memphis & Charleston Railroad and took shares of stock as payment. He supported local schools and dabbled in politics. By 1860 however, as the possibility of war seemed eminent, he was torn, along with his neighbors, about what the future held. He was against secession, but when war was declared, he had no choice but to back the decision of the State of Alabama.

Jim's oldest son Robert left to fight for the Confederacy. Jim traveled to see him at his camp near Shiloh in April 1862. A few days later, one of the bloodiest battles of the Civil War was fought. Jim had already arrived safely at Seclusion, his plantation in Lawrence County, but within a few days, Yankees surrounded them, taking their mules, horses, cotton, and food. His wife, who was left at the plantation home in Athens, didn't fare any better. The Union soldiers were camped around their house. The slaves had invited them to live in their cabins and soon the food supply was gone. Maria Donnell told the slaves they were free to go, but they would not leave. Maria could not milk the cows or tend to the crops in the fields – she was pregnant. To make matters worse, her daughter, 16-year-old Nannie, was critically ill with scarlet fever.

Jim could not get to Athens because a warrant for his arrest had been issued. He wrote to the men who had been close to him before the war, those who had been in favor of Union, like he was, but when war broke out, he went with the decision of the majority of Alabama while they did not. He asked for their help in getting him permission to cross enemy lines to get to his family.

The people of Athens were made to suffer during the Union occupation by Union General Ivan Turchin, known as "The Mad Cossack." Fighting in his native Russia was much more brutal, and he was more than willing to show his American soldiers how it was done. The residents of Athens learned too. According to some historians, Turchin gathered his men together and informed them, "I will close mine eyes for von hour."

At the end of the hour, it appeared to him that they didn't get his drift. He gathered them together again and impressed upon them what he expected of his men. After issuing his statement one more time, some say for a period of 24 hours, they set out to destroy the town. Official records from the military detail the extent of the damage. Businesses were plundered and buildings were burned. Women were raped and soldiers went inside homes to take whatever they wanted. Those who had once pleaded for the South to remain in the union would never feel that way again.

John Haywood Jones, who was Maria Donnell's brother and nearest neighbor, had his new home invaded by soldiers on horseback. They rode through the huge hallway and forced their way in to stay for good. The hams from the smokehouse were sliced on the hand-made carpets, the piano hacked to pieces. Soldiers slept in the family beds, not bothering to remove they spurs and boots.

Maria Donnell watched in helpless desperation as their family belongings were carried off, not because the enemy needed them, but because they could do whatever they wanted. Nannie grew weaker and became upset when she saw the soldiers outside her window, burning their campfires and singing loudly. Her mother asked the commanding officer if he would instruct his men to keep the music low; her daughter was very sick.

"She can go to heaven listening to Yankee music," came the reply.

And she did.

In 1865, the war finally ended, leaving devastation and graves everywhere. Some measure of grief was felt by nearly every family. The Donnells lost their home to high taxes. The older children moved to Texas to start over, and Jim Donnell died before his time. Maria's brother John Haywood Jones, drank himself to death.

The Donnell House entered a new phase. It became a school for young men who lived in the house, as well as their tutors. Over the next few decades, the school had enlarged and outgrew the plantation home. Buildings were constructed around it, and it became the Athens High School. The old home was now the home of the Superintendent of Schools, and many functions, as well as some classes, were held in the Donnell House. By 1970 however, the superintendent had retired and the house was deemed unsafe. Old desks were stored inside while time took its toll on the historic old home. The house was offered to Donnell descendants who would have to pay to have the house moved, but the cost was prohibitive. The old building would have to be torn down for the safety of the students who walked around it.

The historic-minded residents of Athens would not hear of it. A grassroots movement was started to raise money for the repair of the old house. Fund drives, bake sales, fashion shows, and whatever else could bring in a few dollars, were planned to save the old house. Volunteers worked, gave, sacrificed, and saved to have the outside scraped and painted, the columns shored up, the collapsed floors rebuilt, and the walls replastered. Businesses donated money and grants were graciously accepted. It could only be described as a labor of love.

Today the Donnell House is a museum, open for tours and special events. The house is not uninhabited however - there are ghosts there too.

The curator of the Donnell House, as well as many visitors, have had experiences with the ethereal residents. The upstairs room where Nannie Donnell died has a constant uneasy presence. The air is cool and foul-smelling, and most who enter feel anxiety. One can't help but turn their eyes to the window where Nannie looked out to see the Yankee soldiers singing around their fires.

One day, while the curator was cooking something in the kitchen, she felt the tap of someone trying to get her attention. She turned to see that she was alone, however there was instantly a knock on the front door. A very pleasant couple walked in and introduced themselves, and announced that they had a story to tell her.

Some time before, they had been to visit the Donnell House, along with a man who was known to see ghosts, and his daughter who had the same gift. As they walked in the door, they turned to their right to enter the gentlemen's parlor, but were stopped by an austere looking man in old-fashioned clothing, who told them they could not enter. The ghost introduced himself as Reverend Robert Donnell and informed them that they were interrupting his Bible Study class, and would have to wait outside until he was finished. As they took a step back, the ghost of an elderly woman came from the dining room, slapping her hands and clothing. She introduced herself as the Reverend's mother. She explained that she was preparing fresh biscuits for the students who were there for Bible Study.

At this point, the curator stopped the conversation and reminded the visitors that the Reverend's mother had died long before the house was built. Yes, they knew that and had asked the same question, but were told that they had come, as spirits, to the Donnell House long after the property had left the family. The house was finally free of sadness and fear.

When Reverend Donnell had finished his class, he invited the visitors in. Bright sunlight poured into the room that had once been his study, and he stated that it was much too bright for his taste.

The curator explains that the presence she sometimes feels is benevolent and friendly. It isn't difficult however, to go back in time and feel the family's alarm as one imagines the unwelcome intrusion of Union invaders. The girls' room, now decorated with toys from the era, still maintains a deep sense of sorrow.

Today the Donnell House is filled with happiness and celebration. Many events, held in the warmth of a friendly old home and not a sterile conference room, keep the house humming with activity.

Recently, the curator went to open the front door and found that it would not budge. It was unlocked, but no matter how hard she tried to turn the doorknob and force the door open, it remained sealed shut. "Alright Reverend Donnell," she announced. "I'll wait until you are finished with your studies." She waited patiently outside for another five minutes. When she turned the key and tried the door again, it swung easily open.

Confederate General Patrick Cleburne

The Confederate General

Undoubtedly the bloodiest era of our nation's history was from 1861 – 1865, the Civil War. It certainly was anything but civil, and many men and women died years before their time. It's no wonder that there are so many ghost stories concentrating on that period of time; so many souls were left searching, and in sorrow.

The potato was introduced to Ireland in about 1600 and quickly became a staple in many diets. While invading armies destroyed crops and other food sources, the potatoes in the field remained safely underground. Ironically, the food that had once saved the people of Ireland, became the cause of their demise.

The potato famine of 1845 – 1850 decimated the population of Ireland. Peasants, who especially relied on the versatile food item, suffered the most. Those that did not literally starve to death, died of famine-related diseases such as cholera and typhoid. Others emigrated to America and other countries to escape the famine.

One of the thousands that came to America was a man born in Cork County, Ireland on St. Patrick's Day in 1828. Patrick Cleburne immigrated to America in 1849, at the height of the potato blight. His destiny however, brought him to another country's ultimate tragedy – the American Civil War.

As a young man, Patrick Cleburne had enlisted in the British Army. It was a steady job that provided him food and a bed. Patrick hoped to leave Ireland and see the world, but he was dismayed to find his job was to keep order among his own starving Irish countrymen. After three years and seven months in his country's service, he used the money he had inherited from his father's estate to buy his discharge from the British Army and start over in a new country.

Patrick Cleburne settled in Arkansas and became a lawyer. In 1861 however, his adopted country entered the Civil War, and the course of Cleburne's life would once again be ruled by crisis.

Cleburne enlisted in the Confederate Army. His skills learned during his service in the British Army made it obvious from the beginning that he was a leader. Though outnumbered 4-1 against Sherman's army at Chattanooga, he and his men fought with distinction. He again proved himself while fighting against

Hooker's army at the Battle of Ringgold Gap. This time, his men were outnumbered 3 to 1. His heroism was recognized by the Confederate Congress.

Cleburne made a suggestion in early 1864 that was harshly criticized. He proposed a plan to train slaves to fight for the South. In exchange, they would receive their freedom. It was an idea that would solve several problems. Besides having much-needed re-enforcements for the dwindling Confederate ranks, it would also eliminate one of the major reasons for the war.

"Half-trained Negroes have fought as bravely as many other half-trained Yankees," Cleburne said. His idea was rejected.

In the waning days of the Civil War, much of the Southern countryside was laid to waste. Confederate soldiers were starving, the civilians were hungry, and there wasn't enough to feed even the prisoners-of-war. No doubt Major General Patrick Cleburne thought about the correlation to the starving people of Ireland. The irony was that he had left that horror only to find another one.

In late November 1864, Major General Patrick Cleburne stopped at a little church in Maury County, Tennessee. He and his men had marched from Florence, Alabama and their journey would take them to Spring Hill and then Franklin, Tennessee. Cleburne was far away from his home in Helena, Arkansas, and even farther from his native Ireland. He gazed at the small gothic building of St. John's Episcopal Church, near Columbia, Tennessee, and the adjoining graveyard. Cleburne's thoughts probably drifted back to another place named St. John, his ancestral manor house in County Wexford, Ireland.

The small brick church in Tennessee was constructed of slave-made bricks in about 1839. It was a private chapel to the Polk family, relatives of American president, James K. Polk. The church looked like a small medieval castle with a stacked rock wall surrounding the church and the graveyard. Perhaps Cleburne did not know that it was built under the direction of another of his fellow-Confederates – Bishop Leonidas Polk, "The Fighting Bishop."

Leonidas Polk was known to North and South alike, and had graduated from West Point with two other men made famous by the war: Jefferson Davis and Albert Sidney Johnston. Bishop Polk had the little church built on the corner where his property intersected with that of his three brothers. The Fighting Bishop later went to New Orleans to take charge of another parish. In the pulpit as well as on the battlefield, he served his native South.

Bishop Polk was killed by artillery fire at Pine

Ridge, Georgia on June 14, 1864, not long after he had baptized General Joseph Johnston and General John Bell Hood.

Just a few months later, Major General Patrick Cleburne admired Polk's family chapel and turned to one of his men. The quote attributed to him has been written many ways, but in essence says, "I would not mind dying so much if I knew I would spend eternity in such a beautiful place." It was a prophetic remark.

On November 30, 1864, General Cleburne stood with General John Bell Hood at the site that would, in just a few short hours, host a major battle. The night before at Spring Hill, the Confederates expected a successful fight against the Union army, but poor communication between Hood and his officers allowed the Union army to walk silently, in the dark of night, past the Confederates, and on to reinforcements at Franklin. Hood was still angry at the missed opportunity that could have made his career.

Franklin, Tennessee stood in the path to his ultimate target - Nashville. Hood was determined to engage Union troops in battle immediately, against the advice of Generals Cleburne, whom he accused of cowardice, and Frank Cheatham. General Nathan Bedford Forrest advised him on a possible flanking maneuver to avoid a head-on suicidal assault. Hood would not budge from his decision, and he issued orders to attack. He wanted Franklin, Tennessee, and therefore Nashville, in Southern hands again. To wait, in his mind, was to waste valuable time.

General Cleburne was despondent and resigned to what was about to happen. The dark-haired Irishman told his friend General D.C. Govan that if they were to die that day, they should die like men.

Hood's order to General Cleburne was to attack Union General George Wagner's division, not firing until Wagner's advanced line was broken. Cleburne's men were to pursue them to the main Federal line and attack them with fixed bayonets. Hood accused the Army of Tennessee of cowardice, and he insisted he would teach them a lesson in discipline. For too many, that lesson would be their last.

At dusk on the evening of November 30, the carnage began.

As Cleburne's and Brown's men attacked Wagner's artillery, Wagner's men finally broke and ran. The Confederates were fast behind them, led by Patrick Cleburne. General George Gordon and his men were pursuing Wagner's line as well, when General Cleburne raced on horseback toward the enemy, nearly running into General Gordon. Cleburne's horse, Red Pepper, was wounded, and Cleburne quickly took the horse of one of his aides. A cannonball killed the second horse, and Cleburne ran on foot toward the Federals, waving his cap which was on his sword. In his other hand, he held his pistol. Confederate General D.C. Govan watched as his friend Patrick Cleburne disappeared into the smoke, dust, and darkness.

The booming of cannons, the clash of steel, and the explosion of gunfire mingled with the screams of dying men and horses as the stench of gun smoke filled the night sky. The Confederates ran toward the enemy, knowing death was imminent, and the earth would soon open up to claim them. At about 9 o'clock, the horrors of war finally stopped for the night.

Against everyone's better judgment, General John Bell Hood had ordered 25,000 Confederates on a suicidal assault against an army of 35,500. Over 9,500 men on both sides were killed, wounded, or captured, with Southern losses by far the heaviest.

The slaughter at Franklin hastened the death knell of the Confederacy.

Early on the morning of December 1, search parties looked for the wounded and missing. The bodies were so thick it was nearly impossible to step around them. Searchers found the body of General John Adams near the Carter family gin. Just a few yards away, they discovered the body of General Cleburne. He had been shot once through the chest. A scavenger had already taken his boots, watch, and other valuables. His hat lay partially over his face, and his sword was with him. The bodies of the two generals were taken to the porch at the McGavock home at Carnton Plantation, which was already filled with the wounded, dying, and dead.

General John Adams and Major General Patrick Cleburne were placed beside the bodies of Generals Otho Strahl and Hiram Granbury. General States Rights Gist had also been killed at Franklin, and General John Carter would die of his wounds a few days later.

John Bell Hood, the disgraced Confederate commander, had ordered six of his generals to their deaths. In addition, one general was captured, and six other generals were wounded. It seemed Hood blamed everyone but himself for the tragedy.

Later that day, Major Robert Donnell from Athens, Alabama wrote a letter to his mother:

"We had a hard battle yesterday evening….a great many men killed. Tommy Peebles I fear is mortally wounded….We move again this evening at 3 o'clock toward Nashville. I am very much fatigued not having slept for two nights. I am still on Gen. Deas' staff…."

Twenty-year-old Tommy Peebles from Mooresville, Alabama, was already dead.

On December 2, Generals Strahl, Cleburne, Granbury, and Colonel Young were buried in Rose Hill Cemetery in Columbia. Chaplain Charles Quintard of the Army of Tennessee felt that the four officers were buried too close to the graves of Union soldiers, and had them removed to another burial site.

In a strange twist of fate, Patrick Cleburne, along with the three other slain officers, was re-buried in the peaceful graveyard at St. John's Episcopal Church in Maury County, Tennessee. Few Confederate officers had been admired as much as Patrick Cleburne, and General Robert E. Lee referred to him as "a meteor shining from a clouded sky."

A few years later, Major General Patrick Cleburne, dead at the age of 36, was re-interred at his adopted hometown of Helena, Arkansas. Cleburne County, Alabama was named in honor of the Irishman in response to a suggestion made by another veteran of the Battle of Franklin. In Franklin, Tennessee, a marker designates the place where his body was found. It is visible from Cleburne Street.

The Carnton Plantation is finally open for tours. Visitors from all over come to hear the sad story of the human slaughter at the Battle of Franklin. Many stories have been told over the years about a tall thin man in a long gray overcoat and felt hat who roams the grounds, but particularly stays on the upstairs porch. The heavy sound of his boots can be heard pacing or walking on the stairs, and the locals say that "The General" is watching over his men, some of whom are buried in the small Confederate Cemetery within sight of plantation house.

According to sources, a key in the door separating the hallway from the porch had to be removed because The General would lock it if it were left. Several people have called out to the man in the long gray coat, not realizing he was a spectre until he vanished.

On one occasion, a psychic told of hearing The General say, "Well, Govan, if we are to die, let us die like men." Patrick Cleburne finds no peace in his death, perhaps because he feels the sorrow of knowing that he was ordered to lead so many men to their deaths. And surely they were smart enough to realize the impossible odds of living through the massacre themselves. But into eternity they rode that day, along with Patrick Cleburne.

The Ghost of Dallas Mill

Long before rocket science came to Huntsville, King Cotton fueled the local economy. Those who didn't own cotton farms or spend endless hours at the back-breaking job of picking cotton, usually worked in one of the local cotton mills.

Huntsville's Dallas Mill was considered to be one of the best employers. It was a tightly knit community, and with houses so close together, people lived almost as if they were one big family. No one locked their doors and folks were happy just to have a job and a place to live. The peaceful atmosphere that went along with the busy hustle and bustle of industrial life all changed in the 1920s however, when an unspeakable tragedy took the life of one of the mill workers. For the next several decades, his ghost was known to walk the halls of the cavernous building - perhaps as a warning of another terrible tragedy yet to come.

The Dallas Mill was finished in 1892 by Dallas Manufacturing Company, which was headed by Captain T.B. Dallas, originally from Nashville, Tennessee. Mr. Dallas was proud of his mill and he boasted in his annual report to the Board of Directors, "The machinery is complete in every respect and fully abreast of the times, being of the most improved pattern and build." Even in 1892, Huntsville embraced technology and prided itself in possessing a progressive spirit. The state-of-the-art textile mill was designed by Lockwood and Green, a Boston architectural firm. The firm designed many cotton mills in the South, mostly paid for by Northern investors who took advantage of good land and cheap labor in the war-ravaged South.

After only eight years, the Dallas Mill was enlarged to the size of 300,000 square feet. It was an impressive and imposing looking building – the length of two football fields! In its heyday, 59,000 spindles hummed and 1,500 looms were operated by over 1,000 employees, most of whom lived in the adjacent village planned and built by Dallas Manufacturing.

It was very loud and hot inside the mill. Because of the extreme noise, workers learned to read lips. They worked in three shifts around the clock. The mill never stopped, and the hum of production could always be heard throughout the village.

Although wages were low and working conditions substandard by today's measures, mill workers were happy to have employment. Houses and cottages provided shelter for the families while mill schools educated their children and company stores sold them whatever they couldn't grow in their small garden plots, also provided by the company. Some even had a place to keep the family milk cow.

The Haunted Dallas Mill
Photo courtesy of the Huntsville Public Library

The Dallas Mill had been a good idea, and by 1901, there were 10 mills in Huntsville. The Lincoln Mill was built adjacent to the Dallas Mill, and soon rivalries between the mill families formed as well. Children from both Lincoln and Dallas Mills would throw rocks at each other. They were separated by a train track running through the two villages. It was an unspoken code among the village youngsters, that these tracks were not to be crossed by the rival children, except of course when game day rolled around.

In 1912, Dallas Manufacturing began a project to modernize the community. Among the many improvements over the next several years was the installation of over 120 toilets in homes. The toilets were a real point of pride for the inhabitants of the community. To flush the toilet, all one had to do was press down on the seat and running water would automatically come down the line. The only problem was that all the toilets were connected and when one was flushed, they all flushed. The mill also added curbs and gutters.

The community itself was growing. In 1921, a YMCA was built and electricity came to some of the homes. Community theaters were opened, streetcar tracks connected the mills to downtown Huntsville, and baseball teams were formed to encourage camaraderie.

It was truly a golden age for investors of the Dallas Mill. Shortly after the end of World War I however, the tide was beginning to turn. Perhaps it was too much competition or the typical post-war economic lull that signaled the beginning of the end. The Great Depression further crippled the economy, but the tragedy of one man's death will stand out in the history of Dallas Mill.

Dallas Mill had two massive coal burners. While one was in operation, the other cooled and was cleaned before being fired up again. The cleaning process was tedious, and while the burner was officially cool, it was never cold. There were certain rooms in the mill where the child employees were never supposed to go, and the boiler room was one of those places. The adults and foremen knew the dangers, but there was always the chance of an accident.

On that tragic day, the man assigned the task of cleaning the cooled burner went inside, but it was much too soon. Chunks of glowing cinders encased the worker in a horrific tomb as he entered the door. Not only was he severely burned, but the huge amount of glowing cinders smothered him. It was an agonizing way to die, and the mill workers were understandably unnerved.

Not long afterwards, there were rumors about a ghost who walked the halls. There were shadows and sounds of an unseen presence, and even face-to-face encounters with the dead man. The foreboding reminder that danger and death from an accident was ever-near was bad enough, now something or someone was not about to let them forget the tragedy and move on. In retrospect, perhaps the ghost of the dead worker was trying to warn his fellow workers of future tragedies that would eventually seal the fate of the Dallas Mill.

Competition from other Huntsville mills and economic problems hastened the end of the Dallas Mill's golden era. The cotton industry was in a recession and mill workers staged strikes in 1934, 1935, and 1937, sometimes for months at a time. An earthquake centered near Memphis left gaps in the flooring and dislodged bricks on the third floor. Finally, the tenant homes were sold off after World War II, and Huntsville's largest mill was essentially out of business in 1949. It officially closed in 1952. The building was sold to Genesco for $175,000. Shortly afterwards, it was opened up for another manufacturing business and it looked like the life of the old mill building was not ready to flicker out. Then in 1978, the building was put on the National Register of Historic Places.

Still, the rumors about the ghost of the burned mill worker continued. The shadows, the sounds of footsteps and unnerving feeling that an unseen someone was near, continued even in this new era and generation. For some employees, the encounters were startling enough that they quit their jobs with Genesco and vowed never to return.

In 1979, a portion of the adjacent Lincoln Mill caught fire. Workers at the old Dallas Mill building felt the heat through their office windows, and were prepared to evacuate if the direction of the wind changed.

Fortunately for them, Genesco, or the old Dallas Mill, was spared.

But not for long.

In July 1991, the Dallas Mill building caught fire. It had long been empty, and there was speculation that a homeless person had set it on fire, whether or not it was an accident would never be known. The blazing inferno roared angrily for two days as Huntsville fire-fighters worked day and night to extinguish the blaze. The five-story historic building was a total loss, and there was fear that what was left of the nearby empty Lincoln Mill would catch fire and burn to the ground as well. Though they knew they could not save the Dallas Mill, fire-fighters were successful in saving the nearby homes.

The Dallas Mill Burns
Photo courtesy of the Huntsville Public Library

The owner of the building had plans to renovate it. He was devastated by the loss. He was quoted in *The Huntsville Times* as he looked at the last stages of the inferno: "It looks like the ruins of Rome with the columns left standing there."

Today, all that is left is a field of charred bricks and portions of the foundation of the cavernous Dallas Mill. One of the old water towers still stands as a silent sentinel in the center of the long gone community of mill workers. One can stand in the vacant field and only imagine the thousands of lives and stories that passed by in the last century, now forgotten with the passing of time. As for the ghost of the dead mill worker who died in a tragic accident in the 1920s, perhaps he knows there is no one left to warn. Then again, maybe he continues to walk the fields, looking to finish the job that cost him his life that day so long ago.

The Mysterious Death of an American Legend

The Natchez Trace has guided travelers between Nashville and New Orleans for over two centuries. In the light of day, the Trace showcases Nature's beauty at her best, but in the dark of night, near the town of Hohenwald, Tennessee, the sounds of a wounded man crying for help sends many frightened visitors, man and beast, out of the night woods.

On an October night, nearly 200 years ago, an incident happened that causes debate among historians to this day. Two shots rang out under a black velvet Tennessee sky near the present-day town of Hohenwald. The echoes reverberated in the dark forest surrounding the Natchez Trace. Mrs. Grinder, who ran an inn for weary travelers, was frightened by the sound of the shots. She waited with alarm and fear throughout the night. When she ventured outside in the morning, Mrs. Grinder discovered Meriwether Lewis, the governor of the Louisiana Territory and famous American explorer, mortally wounded.

Meriwether Lewis

How did an American legend, who had risen to the height of fame, only to plummet to the depths of poverty and despair, come to lose his life mysteriously on an October night in 1809? The answer may never be known. Though history most remembers him for his leadership role in the famous Lewis & Clark Expedition, his death remains every bit as interesting as his life.

Just over six years earlier, in the Spring of 1803, Meriwether Lewis and William Clark prepared for a 28-month odyssey of exploration and discovery. Their expedition to chart the West was difficult and deadly. Their trip, sanctioned by President Thomas Jefferson, was precipitated by the Louisiana Purchase, which doubled the size of the United States. Forty-four men, hand-picked for their strength and skill with a rifle, left Missouri in May 1804 in search of a land/water route to the Pacific Ocean.

With the help of Indian guides (the most famous was the Shosone woman named Sacagawea) the expedition concluded their adventure where the Columbia River intersects with the Pacific Ocean on the Washington/Oregon border. Their only casualty along the way was Sgt. Charles Floyd, who most likely died of a burst appendix.

To the surprise of the many people who had given them up for lost, Lewis and Clark returned to Washington D.C. in September 1806. Over the next few years however, Lewis's family and friends were alarmed to witness his bouts of despondence and hypochondria. He was known to suffer from deliriums associated with malaria, and it was rumored that he contracted syphilis from Indians he encountered along his journey.

Still, President Thomas Jefferson maintained his confidence in Meriwether Lewis and appointed him governor of the Louisiana Territory in 1807. Debts he incurred during further explorations were not covered by the government, and he was in financial trouble. He had not lost all hope however, and in September 1809, 35-year-old Meriwether Lewis left St. Louis, the capital of the Upper Louisiana Territory, to travel to Washington in an attempt to settle the situation regarding his expenses. He then planned to travel to Philadelphia to have the journals of the Lewis & Clark Expedition published.

Lewis suffered another bout of malaria shortly after he departed Philadelphia with James Neeley, his servant John Pernier, and another servant. He stayed near present-day Memphis until he had recovered enough to continue his journey to Nashville on the Natchez Trace.

All of these facts have been offered to explain the many reasons Meriwether Lewis had for committing suicide. Still, the evidence that suggests murder are as numerous and convincing.

The Natchez Trace was a dangerous road in the early days. Bands of thieves and murderers preyed on lonely travelers and many men simply vanished from the face of the earth while traveling on the Trace. The "Devil's Backbone" as it was known, was little more than a path in some places along the route. It was widely known that there was safety in numbers, and only foolish people traveled the road without companions.

While the men were camped out, one (or two) of their horses ran off. It was agreed that Neeley and Pernier would try to find the horse while Lewis went on ahead to the next inn for travelers, the Grinder home. According to Neeley's recollection, Pernier, the servant, and Lewis went on ahead, while Neeley stayed behind to find the horses.

Lewis arrived ahead of the others, near the present-day town of Hohenwald, Tennessee. Priscilla Grinder (recorded as Griner in some accounts) witnessed Meriwether Lewis rant somewhat incoherently as he paced about the cabin. In one report, she claimed that he left the cabin and she heard shots fired outside. In a different account, she claimed the shots were fired in the room where he was lodged. She said that he had called out for water, but being afraid after hearing the shots, she would not go out to help him. He supposedly even dragged himself to her door and then tried to get water for himself at the well.

The next morning, Mrs. Grinder found Meriwether Lewis, mortally wounded in his bed, in time to hear his final words, "I have done the business my good servant, give me some water." A different version has him saying, as his last words, "I am no coward, but it is hard, so hard to die."

In a different version, she said that she found Lewis outside on the Trace, and confronted his servant who was wearing the clothing Lewis arrived in. This particular version would appear to point the finger at the servant.

There was one thing she had no explanation for, however. Lewis's wallet was empty.

James Neeley appeared sometime later and wrote his account of what happened, although he had not been there to witness the death of his friend Meriwether Lewis. He wrote to President Jefferson that Lewis had committed suicide, and apparently it was an accepted story, not only by the President, but by all the world in general.

Rumors began to surface and several people were accused of murder. Mrs. Grinder's story changed slightly with every telling and she, as well as her husband, remained high on the list of suspects. Her husband claimed to have been several miles away working on the farm at the time of the death.

James Neeley was even accused of either committing the murder or having it done. The reasons ranged from robbery to political assassination. Still another version says a locally known criminal by the name of Tom Runions was responsible for the death of Meriwether Lewis.

Lewis's wounds are rather questionable as well. Some accounts say his head was grazed by a bullet, others say his forehead was partially blown away. Another gunshot wound was found in his chest, though some accounts say it was his side, his back, or even his abdomen. One rumor was that he slashed himself with a razor after shooting himself.

All possible explanations are more than a little bizarre.

John Pernier, Lewis's servant, went to Virginia to see Lewis's mother. He supposedly asked her for $240 that Lewis owed to him, and she chased him away with a rifle, accusing him of her son's murder. Pernier committed suicide seven months later.

Still the most likely suspect would appear to be the Grinder family. Mrs. Grinder's very suspicious explanation of events, along with the fact that her story changed from one telling to the next, would logically suggest that she was hiding something. According to neighbors, the Grinders were very dangerous people, and the neighbors backed up the Grinder story in order to avoid retaliation.

Still more questionable was the fact that the Grinder family bought property and slaves in another part of the state. Where the money came from was always a question. Another strange coincidence is that the location of Lewis's grave, near the former location of the Grinder home, is surrounded by other graves as well. Could they have also been lone travelers on the Natchez Trace?

Perhaps it was no coincidence at all that so many people met their deaths near the Grinders' home. It wouldn't have been the first time that a seemingly benevolent host turned on a lone traveler for money. The Grinders may not have known who their prey was on the last night of Lewis's life. Assuming he was a wealthy man by his clothing and his actions, the Grinders may have killed him and robbed him, hoping no one would miss him. After his hasty burial, Mrs. Grinder could have hastily constructed an acceptable story regarding the events of his death.

Still more curious was the disappearance of Lewis's personal possessions. His gold watch was discovered in Louisiana and his personal papers were sent to his family by an anonymous person 30 years after his death.

The grave of Meriwether Lewis remained unmarked

for 40 years, although the local people remembered the exact location. In 1848, his remains were moved and properly marked. The Tennessee legislature had his remains examined and it was concluded that he was murdered.

Nearly 200 years after his death, there are so many "facts" about the event that it is difficult to sort out myth from reality. That in itself is suspicious. History books have recorded Meriwether Lewis's death as a suicide, but few who have any knowledge of the event are willing to accept it. Though efforts have been made to exhume his remains, if indeed there are any left, the National Park Service has refused to grant permission. Employees stationed near the grave are tight-lipped about the mysterious death as well. They will only concede that he died there and is buried there.

In 1925, President Calvin Coolidge declared Meriwether Lewis's grave-site a national monument. Today the grave of Meriwether Lewis, located near Milepost 385 on the Natchez Trace Parkway, is marked prominently with a huge broken shaft – the symbol of a life cut short.

Even on a bright and sunny day, the area where Meriwether Lewis' grave marker stands is a dark and gloomy place. Visitors to the site report that it seems as if a veil covers them, making them alert to the sounds around them. Even the birds seem to cry out mournfully.

The area no longer has night visitors and even the park service personnel prefer not to go there alone. On still nights in particular, it has been said that one can hear the sound of gunshots ring out, the cry of a wounded man, and his pitiful pleadings for water. It could be Meriwether Lewis re-enacting his last night on earth. But then again, it could be one of dozens of others who met their fate in the same manner - at the hands of the bloodthirsty Grinder family.

Lincoln's Ghost

Queen Wilhelmina of the Netherlands was visiting the White House in Washington, the palatial residence of every American president since John Adams. She had settled comfortably into the Rose Room for the night, when the quiet was disturbed by a knock on the door.

Queen Wilhelmina opened the door to find that her visitor was President Lincoln himself. She looked up at the gaunt face of the tall man. And then, she fainted dead away.

President Lincoln had been dead for over 70 years.

It was not the first time the ghost of Abraham Lincoln was reported to have made an appearance, nor would it be the last. No other American president has had to face the personal and professional turmoil experienced by Abraham Lincoln. He lost two of his young sons to premature death and his wife was plagued with mental instability. He worried for the safety of his son

Robert, who was an officer in the Union Army. His country was in the final stages of the worst crisis in American history. Some people feel that Lincoln's ghost walks this earth because of unfinished business.

President Abraham Lincoln

Students of psychic phenomena agree that Abraham Lincoln had supernatural ability himself, and several incidents seem to support this. After his election, but before he took the oath of office, Abraham Lincoln was sleeping in his room one day when he woke up and looked across the room into a mirror. He saw the image he had come to expect, but next to that was another fainter version of the first. He was startled, and could find no explanation for the haunting image. The next day, the incident was repeated. It was his wife Mary who offered an unusual interpretation of the event. She said it was a sign that Lincoln would live safely through his first term in office, but he would not survive a second term.

President Lincoln frequently had a dream that he was on a swiftly moving ship. In the distance was a dark shore, but the dream ended before he reached the destination. He dreamt it many times in the dark days of the Civil War, and it always preceded the announcement of important news. Before crises in battle, Lincoln came to regard the dream as a sign of impending good news.

During a cabinet meeting on April 14, 1965, General Ulysses Grant spoke about the surrender of Lee's army and the aftermath. No word had been received from General Sherman, who was in North Carolina attempting to track down Confederate General Joe Johnston and his army. Everyone was anxious to hear from Sherman and hoped for details that the largest part of the Southern army had finally surrendered. President Lincoln remarked that, just the night before, he had had the dream about the sailing ship. He interpreted it to mean that they would receive good news from General Sherman. General Grant reminded the president that he had also had the dream on the eve of bad news as well, such as the Union defeat at Stone River.

President Lincoln and his wife were looking forward to a relaxing evening at the theater that night. They had invited several people to attend Ford's Theater with them, including Ulysses Grant and his wife Julia. But Julia Grant woke up on the morning of April 14, 1865 and felt an unusual sense of foreboding. She pleaded with her husband to leave town with her that day, but General Grant reminded her that the cabinet meeting had been delayed until 11 a.m. and that would probably keep them in Washington until the next day.

An invitation was delivered to Mrs. Grant later that day asking that she and the general accompany President and Mrs. Lincoln to the theater that night. Mrs. Grant quickly declined and became adamant that she and her husband leave town immediately. She sent word to General Grant to come home right away, and she was able to convince him of the urgency to leave town. When they arrived in Philadelphia by train, the Grants learned of the President's assassination and of the attempts on the lives of the cabinet members as well. Worst of all was the realization that General Grant was one of the intended victims of the assassination conspiracy.

The most prophetic of all of Abraham Lincoln's visions happened shortly before his death. He told his wife and close friend that he was asleep and dreamt that he heard subdued sobbing throughout the White House. In his dream, Lincoln wandered the halls, but could not find anyone to ask what has happening. He walked into the East Room and saw a coffin with soldiers stationed around it. The face of the corpse was covered, and he could not see who had died. There were many mourners in there as well, and when he asked a soldier who in the White House had died, he was told that the president had been killed by an assassin. A loud wail came from the crowd, and the president was awakened from his most disturbing nightmare.

With the official announcement on the early morning of April 15, 1865 that the president had died, Mrs. Lincoln is said to have anguished, "His dream has come true!"

And so it came to pass, that in real life, the body of Abraham Lincoln was placed in the East Room, and the White House was draped in black crepe for mourning. The undertaker from Alexander & Bryan was called to prepare the body, just as he had prepared the president's young son Willie for his burial in 1862. The undertaker's preparation of Willie had been so remarkable that President Lincoln had his son brought up from his grave so he could look upon him two more times.

Lincoln's body was dressed in a suit he had only worn one time – on the occasion of his most recent inauguration. Secretary of War Edwin Stanton insisted that the discoloration in Lincoln's face, a result of the head wound that ended his life, remain so that the public could see what the Rebel assassin had done to their president.

Over the years, President Lincoln's body has had some interesting history of its own. Grave robbers once attempted to steal his body to hold it in exchange for the release of a prisoner. They were nearly successful. Lincoln's body has been dug up several times and his coffin opened for various reasons. One boy described Lincoln's corpse many years after his death. His suit was covered with a yellow mold and, except for the fact that his eyebrows were gone, he looked just like his pictures in life.

President Lincoln's ghost was reported to have made several White House appearances during periods of national crisis. While he was a guest at the White House, Winston Churchill's suite of rooms included Lincoln's private office. The story is that late one night, after stepping out of the bathtub, Churchill walked naked into the adjoining room. Standing at the fireplace was the specter of Abraham Lincoln.

"Well, Mr. President," Churchill is reported to have said, "You seem to have me at a disadvantage."

With that, Abraham Lincoln vanished.

Others are said to have seen his ghost as well. An employee of the White House claimed to have seen Mr. Lincoln sitting on his bed pulling his boots on. Eleanor Roosevelt and President Theodore Roosevelt claimed to feel his presence on several occasions. Pet dogs belonging to several presidential families refused to enter the room known as Lincoln's Bedroom.

One of President Lyndon Johnson's daughters complained that the phone in her room would ring in the middle of the night and no one was there. She called the White House operator to find out who was calling, only to be told by the operator that no calls had been received.

Other myths have surrounded the shooting death of John Wilkes Booth. For many years, men have claimed to be the real Booth, alive and well. Others profited on his alleged death, and at one time, there were over two dozen skulls traveling about the country with carnivals, all supposedly taken from the body of the assassin.

Eyewitnesses at the Virginia farm of Richard Garrett, where Booth was found hiding in a barn, watched as Union Soldiers torched the barn in an effort to drive him out. The witnesses stated that when Booth refused to surrender, he was shot by a man who claimed he was directed by divine providence. They watched as he was carried from the burning barn to the porch of the Garret house. As his lifeblood soaked into the boards of the porch, Booth asked for someone to hold his hands up in front of his face so he could see them one last time. His spinal cord had been severed when he was shot by soldiers as the barn burned around him. Booth had been paralyzed.

Booth looked at his hands and uttered his final words, "useless, useless." Within three hours, he would be dead.

The next day, men poked through the hot ashes of what was left of the barn. Nothing was left standing except for one solitary pole. The lone pole stood as a scorched reminder of a madman's lost cause.

The officially accepted story is that Booth's body was buried in the same location as the four other conspirators who were tried, found guilty, and executed for the president's death. To dispel rumors that someone other than Booth had been killed, their bodies were dug up and released to their families. When Booth's pine box was opened, his brother Edwin Booth could not bring himself to look at it. He had friends identify his brother's body, and he was buried in the family plot in Baltimore.

Assasssin John Wilkes Booth

Over the years, the porch where Booth bled as he lay dying was said to be permanently stained by his blood. The boards, which had been repeatedly scrubbed, were finally replaced. The house is now gone, a victim of neglect and time.

Ford's Theater is said to have a strange presence as well. Immediately after the President's assassination, Mr. Ford wanted to continue his theater business, but the public would not allow it and the building was gutted. The government paid him for the building and used it for offices and document storage. One day the top floor collapsed, taking all lower floors with it to the ground. Twenty-two people were killed and many more injured. Eventually, it was restored as a theater and to the way it looked in 1865. The presidential box has red, white, and blue swags and even the same portrait of President George Washington that was on the outside wall of the box that historic April night. But no other president has used it to watch a performance. It is believed that, in the course of a performance, any actor who steps across the spot in the floor where John Wilkes Booth landed when he jumped from the balcony, will fumble their line. Employees of Ford's Theater claim to have seen his ghost there as well.

Mary Surratt, the woman hanged for her part in the conspiracy to assassinate the president, is said to haunt the boarding house she ran. Many historians feel her only guilt was that the secret meetings to plan the assassination took place in her home. Still other visitors to her home have claimed to hear whisperings of men as they plotted the conspiracy. Other visitors claim to have seen them huddled together in the back room.

The fate of the young couple who attended the theater that night with the Lincolns is one of the saddest of all. Henry Rathbone, a Captain in the Union Army, was engaged to his step-sister Clara Harris. They both came from prominent families, and became related when Rathbone's mother married Clara's father.

During the assault by John Wilkes Booth, Rathbone struggled with the assassin, and Booth cut him severely with his knife. Because he was fighting with Rathbone, Booth stumbled as he leapt from the balcony, catching his boot on the patriotic bunting attached to the front of the private box. He fell to the stage, breaking his ankle. Despite his injury, Booth stood defiantly, waving his bloody knife as he screamed to the stunned crowd, "The South is avenged!" and then "Sic semper tyrannis!" before he made his painful escape. Booth jumped on the back of a waiting horse and rode off into the shelter of darkness.

Rathbone was said to have blamed himself for the President's death.

Henry Rathbone and Clara Harris finally married in 1867. President Grover Cleveland appointed him to a consulate in Germany and the couple had three children.

On December 23, 1883, Rathbone became enraged and accused his wife of paying more attention to the children than to him. He stabbed and then shot her. When police arrived to find Clara dead, Rathbone said, "Who could have done this to my darling wife?"

Rathbone was found guilty and sentenced to an asylum for the criminally insane. He died in 1911 at the age of 73.

President Lincoln's death left many people, including his country, in a state of unrecoverable chaos. Another of Lincoln's sons died a few years later, and Mary Lincoln was institutionalized for insanity.

The last chapter in the American tragedy of the Civil War began the night of April 14, 1865. The premature death of the 16th president left the nation to wonder what more Abraham Lincoln had to offer his country. If he does wander the earth in frustration over unfinished business, then visitors to the White House may look forward to the specter of Abraham Lincoln for centuries to come.

The Haunted Train Depot

On the early morning of April 11, 1862, the residents of North Alabama slept peacefully, unaware that between four and six thousand Union soldiers under the command of General Ormsby Mitchel had slipped into Huntsville. As a train chugged into the Memphis & Charleston railroad station, preparing to stop, soldiers, dressed in civilian clothing, turned and leveled their rifles at the surprised engineer. With a split second to react, he opened the throttle as the soldiers opened fire. The train sped out and got away.

The next train was not so lucky.

Taking no chances, the Union soldiers positioned a canon to face the track. As the next train slowed down, the soldiers fired the canon, killing a black fireman. On board the train were about 159 Confederate soldiers, on their way back from the Battle of Shiloh.

By 10 a.m., all of Huntsville was aware that they

were now occupied by the Union Army. It had been too easy for Mitchel and his men to overtake the town; all of the men from Huntsville of fighting age were off at war. Other Union forces splintered off to take Athens and Decatur, but the devastation on those towns was far worse.

Of the Confederate soldiers captured at the Depot, those who could walk up to the spacious third floor of the Depot were kept there, under prison guard. Those who were too wounded or sick were kept on the trains still on the tracks. The whole city was tense with worry and fear. It was easy to hate the enemy, yet it was hard; they looked like one of them.

Headquarters of M&C Railroad
Photo courtesy of the Huntsville Public Library

Eventually the walking wounded were turned loose to find their way home. The prisoners on the third floor passed their time by drawing pictures or writing on the walls. They were later sent to Camp Chase to a prisoner of war camp where they would wait to be exchanged or spend the rest of the war in captivity.

Throughout the remainder of the Civil War, the town of Huntsville was under Union occupation several times. Control of the valuable train station was of utmost importance to keep supplies coming and going.

The War ended in 1865 and no one would ever again get back to a "normal" life. The Memphis & Charleston Railroad line went out of business and the Huntsville station was taken over by Southern Railroad. For the next 100 years, it was once again the hub of activity. It was a place to while away the long hours of a hot day, watching the people who came and went. It was the place to see the first public indoor toilet and watch the water flush. Whole families would come to greet a favorite aunt or sadly send off a brother to fight in a far-off war, always with a pronounced farewell, "We'll see you soon!" in hopes it would be true.

The faces changed with the passage of time, hairstyles and clothing styles changed too, as did the wars men left to fight. Men were carried out to fight in the Cuban War, World War I, World War II, Korea, and finally, Vietnam. Not all of them returned. For too many families, their last image of the young man was waving good-bye as he tentatively stepped up onto the train.

Famous people passed through as well, presidents, actresses, suffragists, military leaders, and regular folks. All left an imprint of emotion and a memory.

In 1968, the last passenger train stopped at the Huntsville Depot. The three-story state-of-the-art (in 1860) building was abandoned and neglect began to take a toll. Plans were made for its demolition to make way for a new freeway.

Ah, but the people of Huntsville had a different idea. They would picket City Hall if they had to, but the Huntsville Depot would not be destroyed. It was restored to the way it looked when Southern Railway took it over, repainted yellow and green, the company colors, and opened as a tourist attraction. Today it is a popular stop for school children, history buffs, train buffs, and Civil War students. But occasionally, visitors see more than they counted on – visitors from another era.

Although the ghost stories are not part of the planned tour, tour guides will answer questions about the sightings when asked. Some of them have first-hand experiences with the ghosts.

The third floor seems to hold the most intrigue for visitors. One young woman reported a wall of flame in the corner room. In the same room, a small bust of a Civil War soldier's head is on a pedestal. The head swivels readily when manually moved, but oftentimes it swivels on its own. Depot employees have noticed that at times it will be turned as if gazing out the window and if they pass by a few minutes later, it will be turned as if watching for someone to come in the doorway. One intuitive employee, who had personal experience with ghosts, would not go to the third floor.

A ghost looks down from the second floor window
Photo courtesy of the Huntsville Public Library

Visitors have seen chairs rocking on their own in the children's area, and while a meeting was held one night in a nearby building, attendees saw a ball of flame fly out of the window and hit the ground below, only to disappear.

Other visitors, as well as at least one employee, have seen a man dressed as a railroad worker pace up and down the old passenger platform as if waiting for the train to slow down and stop.

Even stranger still was the elderly woman from up North who came to the Depot on a chartered bus tour. She had an overwhelming feeling that her father was with her when she walked in the door, and although neither of them had been to the Depot or even to Huntsville, she sat and cried uncontrollably for one hour. Her father had died when she was a young girl.

It would be difficult to pinpoint who is haunting the Depot or even what era the spirits are from. Although the building has strong ties to the Civil War, those four years, no matter how traumatic, are only a fraction of time in the life of the building. It would not be surprising to think that a railroad man would still walk the halls, after all, railroad men were there for more than a century.

The Haunted Lodge

The Masonic fraternity has been steeped in mystery since the beginning. Although Freemasonry is believed to have started in London in the early 18th century, many of the customs are believed to have much older origins. The very nature of the organization, with its secret codes and passwords, makes it fertile breeding ground for rumors and suspicion.

The original masons were actually skilled craftsmen – *stonemasons*. Those men who traveled from town to town in Europe were welcomed by their fellow craftsmen and so the organization began and evolved to what it is today – a place to learn the moral teachings excerpted from the Bible and practice benevolence and charity in the community.

Perhaps the shroud of suspicion is an overflow of earlier religious fraternities where one's very life depended on the secrecy of its members. It could be that members enjoyed the men-only nature of the organization. Carrie Nation, the American crusader against alcohol, railed against the Masonic order. Her own husband was a member and she blamed the Masons for the destruction of the family unit. Some historians have suggested that Carrie's personality may have played a bigger role in her husband's extreme interest in the Masonic order!

During the Civil War, some Southern plantations were spared from the torch when Union officers discovered their Confederate enemies were brethren in the lodge. No doubt many lives were spared for the same reason. Throughout the history of the Freemasons, members, often wearing discrete jewelry with the compass and square, have found refuge in times of trouble from other members.

Until the encroachment of the television, the Masonic organization enjoyed an abundance of members. Prominent men found a place to network and forge symbiotic relationships. Active recruiting is not permitted, and so a potential member must ask to receive the rites. George Washington and Benjamin Franklin were among the many prominent men who joined the lodge. All across the country, Freemasons have traditionally promoted civic duty and progress.

Inside the lodge, non-members are perplexed by

the many items of symbolism and placement of chairs. Members will neither confirm nor deny any speculations and their ritual is memorized to be passed from one member to another in one-on-one sessions.

Helion Lodge No. 1 in Huntsville, Alabama is the oldest lodge in the state. On August 28, 1812, Madison Lodge, the forerunner of Helion Lodge No.1, was granted a dispensation from the Grand Lodge of Kentucky and a charter to operate. Alabama Lodge No. 21 was formed on April 6, 1818 under dispensation from the Grand Lodge of Tennessee. In 1822, Alabama Lodge No. 21 became Bethesda Lodge No. 2 and finally in January 1825, the two lodges combined to form one single lodge under the name Helion Lodge No. 1.

Prominent men, settlers of the territory, enjoyed membership and one of the frequent visitors was a tall Tennessean named Andrew Jackson. Helion Lodge No. 1, on the corner of Williams Street and Lincoln Street, was founded by many men who helped forge Huntsville as well as the State of Alabama. John Hunt, namesake of Huntsville was a member, as were LeRoy Pope, known as the Father of Huntsville and several future governors. Several signers of Alabama's first constitution were members, and even Leroy Pope Walker, the Secretary of War for the Confederacy who ordered the first shot fired at Ft. Sumter was a member.

The original building was built for $5,889.12 ½. The cornerstone was laid on November 22, 1823, but the building would last less than 100 years. In 1917, a cornerstone was laid on the new building in the same location, retaining the north wall of the old one. The new building would be attached to the old one so as not to interrupt the business of the lodge, and the old building would eventually be torn down. That decision came in 1920 after a windstorm took down one of the old walls, and so it was razed and the north wall sealed. Inside the lodge today, a stairway goes up to a door in the north wall, which would open into thin air. But it is sealed shut, further adding to the mystery.

On the second floor landing is a huge full-length painting of George Washington wearing the traditional Masonic apron. It was painted in the 1840s by another Mason, Huntsville portrait artist William Halsey. Halsey's paintings are quite rare today and very much in demand.

Pictures of the Past Masters are framed in the dining room with identifying brass plates in chronological order of their terms of office. The photograph of Thomas Taylor, a judge and writer, shows him in his Confederate uniform. He had been a prisoner of war held at Johnson's Island near Sandusky, Ohio. Marmaduke Williams, the first Past Master, was also a delegate to the Constitutional Convention of 1819 held in Huntsville. He ran unsuccessfully for the office of Governor, then served in the House of Representatives for many years. But it is the picture of Past Master H. C. Pollard that most members of the lodge remember. He served five terms in the early 1900s as Past Master. His picture also hangs on the wall alongside the others, but some believe his death did not end his activity in the lodge!

On several occasions, and witnessed by several different people, the brass plaque under Mr. Pollard's picture has popped off. It didn't slide off, or fall down, it literally popped off! Most often it happens when only two or three men are there to witness it, and sometimes it happens when something significant is discussed. One witness stated the picture itself came out of the wall. Oh, and the pictures are *bolted* into the wall.

Others believe one of the ghosts is that of a man who served as Past Master in the late 1960s. He died in the lodge of a heart attack and during later restoration of the building, his name was discovered written on a 2 x 4 under some paneling.

Whoever the person or persons are who haunt the lodge, many people have witnessed doors that open by themselves, a rush of cold wind coming from the locked front door, and doors that slam shut by themselves. While meeting one-on-one with lodge members in the downstairs area, some men have heard the distinct sound of slow footsteps upstairs above their heads. From the sound, they are also able to determine where the footsteps begin, as well as where they end, directly over their heads! One member stopped in disbelief and looked at his instructor when this happened. His teacher looked up at the ceiling, took a drag from his cigarette, and said, "continue." No explanation was offered.

One member once took a date inside to pick something up. The young woman asked him, "Who is that staring at us?"

He was perplexed. "What are you talking about?" he asked.

"The man standing in the corner. Why does he stare at us?"

The young man looked into the dark corner of the hallway and admitted that he did not see anyone, yet his hair stood up in alarm. They immediately left the building and when he regained his composure, he asked her what the ghost was wearing. She described him as well dressed, but his clothing was from an earlier era.

On numerous occasions, Masons have reportedly seen lights on in the third floor of the building when no one was supposed to be inside. One member stopped his car late at night and went inside to turn the lights off. When he got inside, the lights had been turned off. He did not stay long to investigate.

Many men have witnessed the strange happenings in Helion Lodge No. 1. They have no doubt that the ghost or ghosts inside were once members of the historic lodge and perhaps felt such a kinship with the members and the old building that they are reluctant to leave. The presence does not feel sinister, but it has been described as watchful, and certainly uncomfortable. Perhaps the ghosts are simply doing what masons have done through the ages, watch over each other with benevolence and care.

**A ghost watches from the corner
at Helion Lodge Number 1**

The Ghost of Smyrna

In the quiet dusk, a lonesome man with a long white beard walks the grounds of the Davis farm in middle Tennessee. The shadowy figure makes his rounds and watches until the continuing darkness envelopes him. That same figure seems to be summoned by the early morning fog as well, and he continues to walk - looking, searching, perhaps waiting. But he isn't alone.

The two-story home, built on the banks of Stewarts Creek by Moses Ridley, was typical of the prevailing architectural style in 1820. Four columns flank the center porch, a simple railing outlines the upstairs balcony, and the downstairs rooms have traditional high ceilings while the upstairs ceilings are lower for practicality. It was on this 168 acre farm that Charles and Jane Simmons Davis established their family roots when they purchased it from the Ridley family.

Their oldest son Sam was born on October 6, 1842.

He attended school in Smyrna until his enrollment in Western Military Academy in nearby Nashville. He had not spent much time in school when the United States became embroiled in the terrible war against itself – the Civil War. Sam was a restless young man and joined the army even before the state of Tennessee seceded.

Sam Davis was a member of Co. I of the 1st Tennessee Infantry Regiment. Their initiation into the ugliness of war happened at Cheat Mountain in Virginia under their distinguished commander, Robert E. Lee. The 1st fought again at Shiloh, Perryville, and near Sam's own home at Stones River.

Sam was recruited by his older half-brother John into Coleman's Scouts in 1863. By all outward appearances, they were regular Confederate soldiers. They wore gray uniforms, but their assignments were limited to more subversive activities such as intercepting Union communiqués. It didn't take long for Coleman's Scouts to come into the radar of the Union Army, and they were considered to be no less than spies.

In November 1863, a stalemate was in place at Chattanooga. Confederate General Braxton Bragg and his men waited cautiously as Union General Ulysses S. Grant and his men prepared for their next move. General Bragg assumed that Grant was waiting for reinforcements, and he needed to know how many and how soon in order to make his next crucial move. General Bragg sent out men on an expedition to find out what they could. Among the members of that expedition were some of Coleman's Scouts.

On or about November 19, Sam Davis was riding alone on Lamb's Ferry Road near Minor Hill, about 15 miles south of Pulaski, Tennessee. Two men in Confederate uniforms confronted Davis, and although he was in his Confederate uniform, they threatened to conscript him, accusing him of being a runaway. Even though the success of the mission relied on utmost secrecy, Davis felt he had no choice but to explain to the Confederates that he was on a special mission for General Bragg. He presented his pass, signed by E. Coleman, head of the notorious Coleman's Scouts.

It was a fatal mistake.

The two Confederates were actually agents for Union General Grenville Dodge, stationed in Pulaski. Dodge had been directing intelligence operations, including counterespionage. Sam Davis, with his connection to Coleman, was now a big juicy fly caught in the Union Army's web.

The 21-year-old Confederate spy was arrested and taken at gunpoint to Dodge's headquarters for questioning. With fear mounting with each passing second, Davis waited as a thorough search of his saddle and cavalry boots revealed valuable information intended for General Bragg. One message written mostly in abbreviations, would have informed Bragg that General Dodge's headquarters were at Pulaski, while his main force was spread out from there to Lynnville. Others were camped at Elk River and two regiments were in Athens. General Dodge was shocked to see that a handwritten copy of his monthly report had been made from the original on his own desk. He suspected that a former slave named Houston, who had offered his services in Dodge's Army, had provided the report. Also included were 11 newspapers and information on troop movements near Nashville.

Sam Davis was taken to jail and crossed paths with another prisoner. Their glance had been brief, but it was no small incident. Sam Davis was in the same prison with Captain Henry Shaw, *aka E. Coleman*, the leader of Coleman's Scouts. Neither man revealed recognition of the other.

Over the next few days, Henry Shaw/E. Coleman learned that Grenville Dodge himself had interrogated Sam Davis regarding the identity and location of the leader of Coleman's Scouts. Dodge was growing fond of the young man; he was "a fine, soldierly looking young fellow" in his words, and his bearing indicated that he was honorable, noble, and educated. Dodge offered him his freedom if he would only give up the name of his leader. Davis refused, though Dodge continued his efforts in hopes of wearing him down. Meanwhile, in another part of the jail, Captain Henry Shaw knew his fate would be sealed if General Dodge succeeded.

The Union soldiers had no idea that Henry Shaw was the brilliant and elusive leader of the band of scouts. Though the reasons were somewhat unclear, Shaw had been taken into the Pulaski jail by Union soldiers. They had described him as "an old, seedy, awkward-looking man in citizen's clothes" and he had admitted only to being a former surgeon for the Confederacy. For seven days Sam Davis was interrogated and for seven days, Henry Shaw waited for him to break his silence and in essence sign Shaw's death sentence with his admissions.

General Grenville Dodge was now pleading with the young man that he had grown to admire. He wanted to let the young man live, but he was bound by the military rules he had taken an oath to abide by for the sake of the United States. Because Davis had continually refused to give Shaw up, Dodge had no choice but to send him to the court martial board.

On November 24, Sam Davis pleaded guilty to being a courier, but not guilty to the charge of being a spy. Still, he was found guilty on both charges and sentenced to die on the gallows. The young man who should have had a long and promising life ahead of him had three days left to live.

On the evening of November 26, Sam wrote to his mother, "I have got to die tomorrow morning. Mother, I do not hate to die." He also left instructions for them to retrieve his body so he could be permanently buried at his home in Smyrna.

On the morning of November 27, the young prisoner was taken from the Giles County Jail and placed on a wagon that would carry him to a hill overlooking Pulaski. His seat? The coffin his lifeless body would lie in. The citizens of Pulaski knew of the young man and his execution. They had hoped, as did General Dodge, that he could somehow be spared. As the wagon bearing the young man and his coffin approached the scaffold, the townspeople respectfully closed their shutters and doors so as not to turn his death into a spectacle. Only a young girl, who had escaped the watchful eye of her mother, ran outside to watch the gloomy procession up the hill.

As the noose was placed around his neck, General Dodge asked him once again to give him the information that would grant Sam Davis his life. His last words would seal his fate, "I would die a thousand deaths before I would betray a friend."

With a feeling of prevailing sadness, Dodge ordered the shroud placed over his head and he then gave the nod. The trap door was sprung. Young Sam Davis's body fell through the hole until the rope stopped his fall, snapping his neck instantly.

Sam Davis was buried in Maplewood Cemetery. In a few days, his father and younger brother would arrive with another coffin for Sam. He was taken back to his home and his body was kept in the parlor for a few days while friends and loved ones said their final good-bye. No one suffered as much as his grief-stricken mother.

Henry Shaw must have felt relief mixed with regret. He knew that his life was traded for that of Sam Davis. He survived the Civil War. General Grenville Dodge survived as well, though he was severely injured in 1864.

Years later, a grassroots movement was started to establish a permanent reminder of Sam Davis's hero-ism. A collection was started for a monument in Nash-ville, one of several memorials to the martyr. A man in his 70s made a $10 contribution toward the memory of Sam Davis. His name was Grenville Dodge. Dodge had not been the only Union soldier to admire the young man from Tennessee. Letters from his captors offered admiration for the brave Confederate.

Though there are several markers, monuments, and museums to honor the young man, his own home holds the most personal significance. It is now open for tours and hundreds of school children visit to learn more of Tennessee's extensive Civil War history. Perhaps the ghostly happenings are easily overlooked in the excitement of these visits from the eager young scholars. But when the grounds are silent and the air is still, the tour guides have sometimes heard the sorrowful cries of a grieving mother coming from the parlor. House keys are strangely useless when the guides try to enter the house, yet when a sufficient amount of time has passed, perhaps when the grieving is over for now, the keys open the locks, as they always have before. It is not uncommon to feel an invisible presence in the old home, and the sadness that filled the home in the war that was anything but civil, is still evident.

As for the shadowy figure of the man who walks the grounds, employees believe him to be the younger brother of Sam Davis who was the last of the family to live there. Perhaps he can't bring himself to leave the home he knew all his life or maybe he, along with other members of his family, remain at the Smyrna, Tennessee home to help keep the memory of his brother Sam from fading into history.

Massacre at Ft. Mims

August 30, 1813 was oppressively hot. The residents of Ft. Mims, both military and civilian, moved slowly in the early morning heat. In the Baldwin County outpost near Mobile, most days were uneventful, and this day was expected to be like every day before.

Major Daniel Beasley was in charge of the stockade which housed about 550 settlers, slaves, militia, and half breeds. There were some 17 buildings inside the fenced area which was protected by about 120 men. The fort had been established for just over a month, and because it was already overcrowded and built near a swamp, many of the residents were sick.

About 30 miles northwest of Fort Mims was another post – Fort Easley. Rumors were spread that the Creeks were planning to attack Fort Easley, and an additional 80 men were sent there for reinforcement. Everyone waited anxiously. Mount Vernon, located a few miles west of Fort Mims, had received 50 of the Fort Mims soldiers, leaving only 70 soldiers to defend Fort Mims.

Major Beasley had no military experience, but his friend General Ferdinand L. Claiborne lobbied to have him appointed as a militia major, and he had come to Fort Mims in early August. Major Beasley sat down to write a note to General Claiborne describing a false alarm the day before, started by slaves who claimed they had seen Indians with war paint, "committing every kind of Havoc" while on an expedition to buy corn at a nearby plantation. Beasley, in response to the slaves' alarm, had sent out ten soldiers on a scouting expedition, as a precaution, to confirm the rumors. They returned, having seen no Indians. Beasley ordered that the two slaves be whipped for lying. One was flogged, the owner of the other refused to allow his slave to be whipped because he believed his story. Beasley described his reaction to the false alarm:

"I was much pleased at the appearance of the Soldiers here at the time of Alarm yesterday when it was expected that the Indians would appear in Sight, the Soldiers very generally appeared anxious to see them."

Even as he wrote those words, the Creek Indians, also known as Red Sticks, were gathering in the woods outside the fort. Between 750 to 1000 warriors had finished applying war paint. Chief Red Eagle, known also

133

as William Weatherford, had planned an attack. Some of the braves had rifles that had been provided to them by the British stationed at Pensacola, specifically to kill the Americans.

Earlier that same morning, one of the slaves who had seen them the day before, was sent out to tend the cattle. Again, he saw the braves readying for an attack. Rather than return to the fort and risk another beating or death by the Indians, he fled to nearby Fort Pierce.

General Claiborne had been to Ft. Mims for an inspection only weeks before. He had instructed his friend to fortify their defenses and add two or three additional blockhouses. Beasley was not impressed with any urgency and believed they would be safe for some time. A defensive wall was built inside the stockade, facing the main gate, and in his report, Beasley had reported that they were "perfectly tranquil." The additional blockhouses could wait.

"I Have improved the fort at this place and have it much Stronger than when you were here," Beasley wrote.

Beasley was drinking whiskey, which had arrived the day before, as he continued his letter. A scout named James Cornells had rushed into the fort on horseback, and excitedly informed Beasley that hostile Creek Indians were approaching the fort. Beasley ordered Cornells arrested after telling him he had only seen red cows and had assumed they were Indians. Cornells galloped out of the fort on his horse.

Major Daniel Beasley had ignored two warnings that the Creek Indians were about to attack. As he continued his letter and poured another drink, the Creeks were performing a ceremony to make four braves bulletproof. They would lead the attack and be the first to enter the fort.

As the sun rose high into the sky, the air got hotter and the humidity made it difficult to breathe. Some soldiers played cards to pass the time while some of the girls danced. At noon, the call to lunch was sounded by a drummer and the settlers casually made their way to tables. The talk was, as always that time of year, about the excessive heat.

The Indians hid in a ravine only 400 yards away. Another drum roll sounded, this time outside the stockade. It was the signal to attack. The Creek Indian warriors rallied and it took only seconds to cover the ground from the ravine to the open gate of the fort. They were led by the four "bullet-proof" braves who rushed through the gate with lightning speed.

Although caught completely by surprise, the militia reacted quickly. The four braves who had been anointed in the protection ceremony, danced and chanted, believing that the bullets that hit them would split in two and fall harmlessly to the ground. Three of the four were quickly shot, to the surprise of the warriors that followed, and the fight was on. Confusion and surprise gave the clear advantage to the Creek Indians as panicked residents of the fort ran for cover and weapons. Mothers snatched their children and ran as the Indians picked them off with their own rifles. Quickly, the unoccupied blockhouse, which the whites had counted on for safety in an event such as this, was taken by the Indians.

Major Beasley drew his sword, but his reactions had been slowed by whiskey. He tried to close the gate, but the Creeks clubbed him to death. Taking over command was a half-breed named Dixon Bailey, who lived at Fort Mims with his large family. Bailey ordered, time and again, for someone to run to Fort Easley for backup, but everyone refused. Several men took cover behind the buildings and fired at the onslaught of screaming Indian warriors who kept coming and coming. The air was filled with terrifying cries of fallen men, women, and children.

Zachariah McGirth, a resident of Fort Mims, had left with two slaves two hours before the attack to get supplies. From the distance, they heard the gunfire and saw the smoke as it rose from the direction of the fort.

His family was at the fort: his wife, seven daughters, and one son. He watched helplessly from the Alabama River.

The carnage continued for an appalling three hours. Everyone was exhausted, and the casualties for both sides were high. While some Indians had rifles, most had fought with clubs, knives, bows and arrows, and tomahawks. Soon they set arrows on fire and sent them into the buildings where the settlers had taken cover. As the flames engulfed the buildings, women and children were burned alive. Others ran out the doors, only to be scalped by waiting Indians who had heard that the British were offering a $5 bounty for each American scalp. They were killed, *after* they were scalped.

Women and girls were mutilated during the frenzy. Their abdomens were splayed open and unborn babies cut out of pregnant women. The innocent children were killed in ways too horrible to recount. Bodies were thrown into piles and set on fire, some still alive. Even Chief Red Eagle was shocked at the frenzy of the Indians he had led. He left the fort himself when his own warriors threatened him as he ordered them not to kill the women and children.

The residents of nearby Fort Pierce heard of the attack and saw the rising smoke of the burning buildings at Fort Mims. They waited in silence and fear, hoping they would be spared from the same fate. Fort Pierce had a small force of militia and knew they could not help their comrades at Fort Mims. In the stillness of their fort, they could hear the screams of the dying.

Still the fighting continued. One woman who had watched in horror as her husband was killed, took her two children and walked out into the frenzy to end the agonizing wait for death to come to them. Dog Warrior, one of the Creek warriors, took the three to safety – he had known the family and had been treated kindly by them when he was a child.

Dixon Bailey, who had taken over command when Major Beasley was clubbed to death, was killed. His sister was confronted by a Creek warrior who asked who she was related to in the fort. She pointed to the lifeless body of her brother, whereupon the Indian knocked her down and mutilated her before she was mercifully overtaken by death.

At about 5 p.m., the Indians had finished their grisly task. They took slaves, some women and children, and left the ruins of Fort Mims. One soldier who had escaped had hidden in the forest while a portion of the attacking Creeks camped nearby. They had taken four prisoners with them to torture throughout the night. Their bodies were left behind. Another settler, the assistant surgeon, wandered through the woods for nine days before finding safety.

Fearing they would be attacked as well, the residents of Fort Pierce abandoned the outpost and fled to Mobile, about 35 miles away. They arrived safely on September 4.

Four days after the slaughter, a settler returned to Fort Mims in search of his family. He reported that he saw about 250 dead bodies, but some say the death toll was as high as 500. About 20 slaves had been slaughtered and between 100 and 200 were captured by the Creeks. Three weeks later, a detachment of soldiers was sent to bury the dead, all of whom had been scalped, many mutilated. Vultures had been feeding on the corpses. With so many burned, it became impossible to identify who they were or even how many had been burned. Their remains were buried in two large pits.

In the forest surrounding the fort, the graves of the dead Creek Indians were discovered as well. They had been left between the rows of potatoes and half-heartedly covered with vines and dirt before the living Indians, bored with the task, left.

Several months after the massacre at Fort Mims, Zachariah McGirth, who had listened to the carnage from the Alabama River, was surprised to be reunited with his wife and seven daughters. Although he had returned on August 31 to find the bodies of his family, only his son's could be found. His wife and daughters had been saved by a Creek Indian named Sanota, who had been taken in by the McGirths when he was orphaned as a child.

The Creek Indians had won the battle, but not the fight. The Fort Mims Massacre, the worst Indian massacre in history, marked the beginning of the Creek Indian Wars.

Today the site of the old fort is a public park. In the daytime it seems peaceful and pristine, hardly the place for the worst Indian massacre in United States history. Writer Sally Remaley wrote a story about a man named Floyd Boone, who once found himself as an unplanned, and perhaps unwelcome, overnight guest at Ft. Mims in 1966. He and a friend built a fire to fight the chill and settled in for the night. They climbed into their sleeping bags and closed their eyes. It was a good night for sleeping - no wind, no bugs. Soon however, they heard low moans. Neither man stirred, hoping it was their fertile imaginations at work. But then they heard footsteps, along with the moaning that became increasingly louder. The footsteps came closer to the two men and stopped. At this point, both men agreed it would be best to give up their quest for slumber and sit up for the rest of the night.

As they stoked the fire, the drama continued around

them, seemingly oblivious to the presence of these visitors from another century. Six loud drumbeats were heard over the long gone entrance to the east gate at about 1 a.m. The beating of horses' hooves thundered through the cries of dying men, women, and children. The Ft. Mims Massacre was occurring, apparently in the spirit world, all over again.

The eyes of the two men looked in the direction of each horrible sound, but all they saw were the shadows of the night. Each incident in the horrible massacre was unfolding in the order it happened in 1813. The two men were too frightened to move, too fascinated to leave, yet unable to grasp something that could not be seen by their own eyes. At 4 a.m., they heard a drumbeat near the site of the old blockhouse and the ghostly carnage stopped. They sat by the fire until the light of the morning sun transformed the area into a peaceful field once again.

Who can explain the eerie events witnessed by these two men, and maybe many others as well? American Indians have always been spiritual in nature, and perhaps the spirits are reliving a time when their warriors ruled the land, before their children were consigned to reservations far away. But for now, no one will ever know.

The Ghosts of the Alamo

Out of the Indian Wars in Alabama rose several men whose names will be remembered in history. General Andrew Jackson became President of the United States. Davy Crockett and Sam Houston entered politics as well, but went to Texas to find fame and infamy.

This is their story.

Davy Crockett was eccentric, but could spin an entertaining yarn. Unfortunately, he did not appear to enjoy or prosper on his Tennessee farm. He began his foray into politics as Justice of the Peace for Lawrence County, Tennessee in 1817. In 1821 he ran, and was elected, to the Legislature. For the next several years, he was elected, defeated, elected again for the Legislature and Congress both. He was an outspoken opponent of Andrew Jackson however, and it may have even stemmed from an altercation he had with Jackson while they both fought the Indians in Alabama. Crockett was good at self-promotion, and with the help of publicity from several books that were offered as factual accounts of his life, he became known as a bear-hunting, coonskin-cap-wearing cross between the earlier Daniel Boone and later Will Rogers.

David Crockett

Crockett's name had been bandied about to run against Andrew Jackson for President, but in the end, he lost his seat in Congress and his patience with politics. In November 1835, in a Memphis, Tennessee drinking establishment, Crockett raised his glass and made his famous announcement, "...You may all go to hell and I will go to Texas."

Sam Houston

Sam Houston, a native of Maryville, Tennessee, had also enjoyed success in politics. In 1829, at the age of 38,

Tennessee Governor Sam Houston married 19-year-old Eliza Allen. The marriage was over almost as soon as it began, and Governor Sam Houston resigned from office in shame and left the state. History only speculates on whatever scandal caused the dissolution of his marriage, but writer Jim Green of Rociada, New Mexico, a descendant of the young lady from Tennessee, tells us the story as it was passed down in his family.

The governor, nearing middle age, had some wild living and practice at hard drinking in the years behind him. His young bride, a daughter of a former Tennessee governor, had been strongly encouraged by her family to marry Governor Houston. After her wedding ceremony, she was shocked by the coarse language and rowdy manners of her worldly husband. Only days after her wedding, she had had enough and ran scared. Another source reasons that the young bride admitted to her husband that she was in love with another. According to one account, Governor Houston was strong-armed into resigning, but perhaps he was badly shaken from the rejection and came to the decision on his own. Nevertheless, Governor Houston left his position and the state of Tennessee behind him for the western frontier.

Although Sam Houston had his admirers and outstanding leadership qualities, he was also known as pompous, conceited, profane, and way too familiar with liquor. One interesting story regards a meeting between Sam Houston and Davy Crockett in Little Rock, Arkansas. Crockett was escorted into the presence of Houston, who chose that day to receive guests in the nude, save for a newspaper strategically placed in his lap. Crockett, ever a gentleman, did not remark on the Emperor's New Clothes. Later when he recalled the incident he said, "He was in a bad plight to repel mosquitoes."

Several attempts had been made in centuries past to tame the wild frontier of Texas. Spaniards had sent missionaries who tried to introduce Catholicism to the Comanche and Apache Indians. Ownership became a bone of contention in 1803 when France ceded the Louisiana Territory to the United States. The property had belonged to Spain before that, and Spain laid claim to the area east of the Sabine River. The U.S. claimed all the property to the Rio Grande and a settlement was finally reached with the neutral ground established between the Sabine and Arroyo Hondo. Still, the piece of paper did not keep the Americans and Spaniards from killing each other. A Tennessean named Dr. James Long established a provisional government in Nacogdoches and La Bahia, but the inhabitants were murdered by the Spaniards. Dr. Long met his fate when he was assassinated in 1822.

The next year, Stephen Austin established a colony

from a grant by the Mexican government. It was then that every cutthroat, murderous criminal found a home – as long as they would adopt the Catholic faith and re-linquish their American citizenship to become citizens of Mexico. Even the pirate Lafitte settled for a while in Galveston. It was understood that most people took an alias and the saying, "When the other states reject us, this is the one that always 'takes us'" was the tongue-in-cheek origin of the name Texas.

By the early 1830s, Texas was beginning to look good to people willing to settle a new frontier and see the boundaries of America broadened. About 1,000 Americans per month moved into Texas. To Davy Crockett, it seemed like a good place to finally make his fortune and jump-start his political career. He half expected to be elected to serve in the first Constitutional Convention, but historians aren't clear on what his exact intentions were. Undoubtedly, a new beginning in a new country beckoned him. Everywhere he stopped in Texas, he was greeted with crowds of enthusiastic supporters – perhaps future constituents? He took advantage of the excitement and pressed on, hoping he was adding new friends/voters along the way. When he reached the outskirts of San Antonio, he paused and asked that the great Jim Bowie escort him into town. They arrived with much fanfare and celebration.

Hostilities were already heating up between the Mexican government and the Texas Anglos. The area encompassed by Texas was extensive. France, Holland, Belgium, and Denmark together did not equal the acreage in Texas, and the area was 36 times larger than New Jersey. Santa Anna, president of the new republic and Mexico, was the head of the Mexican Army. He was among those who wanted the influx of Americans to stop, recognizing that his authority was in danger. The Texas Anglos soon set up a provisional government in line with their Declaration of Independence. Sam Houston, already active in the revolutionary movement, became the commander-in-chief of the militia.

In December 1835, the Mexicans were driven out of San Antonio, a mission town founded in 1692 by Franciscan friars. Thick adobe walls had been built to protect the Catholic inhabitants from hostile Indians when the Alamo, the Spanish word for cottonwood, was built in 1774. In early 1836, the Mexican Army, under Santa Anna's ruthless leadership, began their march to San Antonio, whose inhabitants now numbered 1,200.

In the meantime, a power struggle was taking place in the American militia. Sam Houston had ordered that the Alamo be razed to keep the Mexicans from taking it over, but his directive was ignored while William Travis and Jim Bowie argued about who was in charge.

Turning to Davy Crockett for support, he told them both that he was content as a "high private."

William Travis was born in South Carolina, but moved with his family to Alabama. He became an attorney and married a Claiborne County girl, but he abandoned his pregnant wife and son to go to Texas. In official documents, he listed his marital status as "single" although he had not gotten a divorce.

Jim Bowie was a native of Tennessee. He was quick to anger, and also to settle a fight through violence. His hotheadedness was tempered by his brother Rezin P. Bowie, who was very close to his famous brother. It was Rezin, some believe, who actually designed the first Bowie knife out of a blacksmith's rasp, which he gave to Jim for protection. Rezin Bowie was his brother's opposite – friendly, open, a good-natured pacifist.

Jim Bowie was widowed by the time he got to the Alamo. He had married Ursalita de Veramendez - the goddaughter of Bowie's enemy, Santa Anna.

In late February, Santa Anna's men were encamped outside the Alamo at a relatively safe distance. Travis and Bowie both sent out representatives to Santa Anna to reach an amicable agreement, and both were rejected. Jim Bowie became gravely ill, some say he suffered from typhoid fever while others have speculated he had pneumonia. Still another source says he was in the end stages of tuberculosis. At any rate, the leadership issue became a moot point and William Travis took over.

Jim Bowie

The siege began. Col. Travis sent an urgent message to Col. James Fannin in Goliad, asking for reinforcements. After several requests, Fannin sent his army, but four miles away, he decided to turn back, leaving the hopeful Texans waiting in anticipation. Desperate for help, Travis went into the town and asked the locals to join in the fight, but they refused. Stranded, desperate, and abandoned by their leaders, they knew what lay ahead - a fight to the death. In the meantime, the

Mexicans tried to cut off the supply of food and water to the Alamo where the men were now living, unaware that the Texans were already digging a well.

Santa Anna demanded unconditional surrender. A cannon shot from inside the fort was the prompt reply. Santa Anna ordered that a crimson flag be hoisted over the tower of Old San Fernando Church. The ominous symbol meant "no quarter" or that all enemies would be put to death.

The civilians of San Antonio left town.

The Mexicans pointed their cannons at the Alamo, measuring the optimum distance by firing them. When one cannon was wheeled too close, Crockett aimed his rifle and shot the Mexican as he tried to light the fuse. He was replaced with another, who was promptly shot by Crockett as well. Another was felled, then another and another before the cannon was moved out of range. Over the next few days, the back and forth fighting continued. About 300 Mexicans were killed by sharp-shooters, with no casualties within the Alamo.

From the town of Gonzales, 30 men arrived to support their brethren in arms at the Alamo. They were received as royalty! Still, a tiny garrison of 183 men had little hope of living through an attack of several thousand Mexicans.

The shelling against the defenders was now constant

throughout the day and night. Davy Crockett worked at keeping the morale of the defenders up. He played his fiddle to the accompaniment of Scotsman John McGregor's bagpipe. He entertained the men with his tall tales and humor. The 49-year-old man, with a lined face that looked much older, refused to let them accept their inevitable fate.

After 11 days of siege, Santa Anna was out of patience. A woman from the town informed Santa Anna that the defenses at the Alamo were about to collapse and she urged him to attack immediately. On the night of March 5, the guns were silent as the Mexican Army rested for the assault. At 4 a.m. on March 6, the Mexican band played *Dequelo*, a fight song that signified there would be no survivors. The bugles sounded the attack and the Americans took their posts at the adobe building.

The bloodbath began. The Americans picked off the first of the Mexicans to reach the walls, but they kept coming, pushing the bodies aside to scale the walls. They came – too many and too fast for the Texans to keep up. Smoke filled the air, the deafening sounds of gunfire and cannon fire mixed with the agonizing screams of death. Blood gushed from bullet, saber, and knife wounds as frantic hands slashed at enemy flesh.

Sixteen-year-old Galba Fuqua was one of the men

who had arrived on March 1. He tried to speak to Susanna Dickenson, a woman in the fort, but his jaw had been broken. The young man from Alabama did not survive, nor did Susanna Dickenson's husband. William Fishbaugh, another native of Alabama who arrived March 1, died as well, as did Alabamian James Buchanan. Fifteen men from England, members of the New Orleans Greys, died that day. Thirty-one from Tennessee were slain, 14 from Pennsylvania and 15 from Kentucky. Most of the Texas natives who died that day bore Spanish and Mexican surnames. Texas and Virginia both contributed 12 lives and New York lost six. They came from Ireland, Germany, Wales, and Scotland. Connecticut, Illinois, Maryland, New Hampshire, and New Jersey contributed one apiece. Scores of others were from unknown places.

Jim Bowie, from his sickbed, waited for the enemy with loaded guns and his famous knife. As the Mexicans rushed in, he fired quickly, each bullet finding its mark. The dead lay around him, but he was mortally wounded. As a Mexican rushed in to finish the kill, Bowie grabbed him by his hair and plunged the blade into his gut. Both men fell to the floor, dead.

By daylight, the killing was over. Some said William Travis and Davy Crockett were among the first to die. Six men had been taken alive, and according to one source, William Travis and Davy Crockett were among them, Crockett was captured with his Bowie knife dripping blood in one hand and the bloody barrel of his gun, with its broken stock, in the other. The Mexican General sent word to Santa Anna asking that the prisoners be delivered to him. Santa Anna was furious and ordered them killed immediately. Crockett, upon hearing the verdict, lunged with his Bowie knife at the nearest Mexican. Before he could make it halfway, his body was riddled with bullets. The others were executed in the same manner.

Santa Anna ordered that the bodies of the Americans be stripped and taken outside the fort. They were stacked intermittently with wood and a funeral pyre was set ablaze. There was one exception however. By order of Santa Anna, the body of his goddaughter's husband, Jim Bowie, was buried in an unmarked grave.

At least 1,000 Mexicans, perhaps as many as 1,600, and 183 Texans perished on March 6, 1836. The battle cry, "Remember the Alamo!" resounded at every subsequent battle until the Texans won their struggle for independence. The ashes of the dead men were gathered into a large box and kept, with reverence, inside the Alamo, today a symbol of Texas pride.

On the day of their death, heroes were born. The fight for freedom, started 60 years earlier by men who fought for America's independence, was written in blood once again, this time on Texas soil.

News of the slaughter was slow to reach the newspapers in the east and south. Jim Bowie's mother was told of her son's tragic death. She remarked that she knew he hadn't died from a wound to his back. Then she returned to her work.

The fact that the Alamo has remained standing for so long may not be entirely because it is a symbol of Texas pride. Martyrs were born on that March day in 1836, the day that their mortal bodies died. The Mexicans realized the potential consequences of leaving the Alamo intact to inflame other rebels. The massacre at the Alamo, although it was a victory for the Mexicans, came at a huge cost of human life. After Santa Anna's capture, General Andrade ordered his men to tear the Alamo to the ground. It would not be a monument to the bravery of the Texans, it would instead be a reminder of the rebels' bloody fate.

Before the actual destruction of the walls, workers took down the gun emplacements along with anything that could be salvaged for use elsewhere. It was now time to knock the walls down. Workers were stunned to find that when they tried to come near the walls, ghostly hands came from inside the walls to halt their work. Six ghostly figures, believed by some to be monks, stand in front of the door with flaming swords in their hands, daring any who enter. A huge entity has been seen coming from the roof with arms outstretched and holding balls of fire in its hands. Lit torches were held in the filmy hands and a voice from another world sent an ominous warning:

"Depart! Touch not these walls. He who desecrates these walls shall meet a horrible fate. Multiple afflictions shall seize upon him and a horrible and agonizing and avenging torture shall be his death!"

Several groups of men were hired at different times to tear down the walls and all left with the same fear, irrational or not. It has been told that one man was entombed alive and burned to death.

These are not the only ghosts believed to be haunting the site. A woman is seen walking the grounds, a man who leans out the window, looks around and then retreats back inside, a large Indian, and a cowboy in a long duster, dripping wet, have also been seen around the Alamo. And so for now, the Alamo will remain standing until the spirits deem the time has come to let the past go.

Aaron Burr's Angry Spirit

On the early morning of July 11, 1804, two boats rowed across the Hudson River to rendezvous at a spot near Weehawken, New Jersey. Two well-known men were meeting for an "interview," a polite term coined for a deadly meeting with guns. Aaron Burr and Alexander Hamilton were about to engage in an illegal duel to the death.

Two brilliant men who fought with distinction in the American Revolution and were personally associated with George Washington found themselves in opposite political arenas. They had once been friends, and now they sought to settle differences by the rules established in the *code duello*, a gentleman's guide to civilized fighting.

How could two men, who had given so much to the fledgling country, come to such a point in their lives? Both men craved power in politics. Aaron Burr had

Alexander Hamilton

served as the third vice-president of the United States, though he had aspired to be the president. When he and Thomas Jefferson received the same amount of electoral votes, the House of Representatives broke the tie, and Aaron Burr, in second place, took the role as vice-president. At the end of his term, he ran for governor of New York, but Alexander Hamilton had campaigned against him and slandered his reputation at every opportunity, helping Burr to lose the election. Burr also suspected that Hamilton had a hand in the vote that kept him from the U.S. presidency.

Aaron Burr demanded a public apology to cover the previous 15 years of ill will between the two men. Hamilton refused. Burr challenged Hamilton to a duel in order to settle their disagreement in a "gentlemanly" manner.

Hamilton accepted. He had high political aspirations as well, but because of an affair with a married woman named Maria Reynolds, for which he was being black-mailed by the woman's husband, his political future had stalled. But soon that wouldn't matter anyway.

Much care had been taken to protect the men, legally, should either survive to face charges in a court of law for dueling. Their assistants, or "seconds" had held umbrellas over their heads to conceal them from the men who rowed them over. Those men had been instructed to turn their heads so they would not witness the actual duel.

Alexander Hamilton brought along the dueling pistols, his right under the code duello. They had been specially made for dueling, and already had an interesting history. Hamilton's son had been killed in a duel, using the same pistols. In yet another duel, Hamilton's brother-in-law had dueled with Aaron Burr himself, and had shot the button off of Burr's coat with one of the pistols. In addition, they were outfitted with a device that set a hair trigger. Only one pound of pressure would fire the gun, as opposed to the usual twenty pounds, making it easier to control the aim of the shooter.

The smooth-bore chamber of each gun was loaded with a .54 caliber bullet. The two men were called together to hear final instructions. Alexander Hamilton felt a sense of impending doom. He had already written a letter of farewell to his wife, to be read in the event of his death. He told his second on the boat trip over that he planned to "throw away" the first shot, meaning he did not intend to aim at Burr at all. When asked if he wanted the hair trigger set, a move that would guarantee his advantage, he refused. And finally, given the first choice of his position, he chose to stand where the sun would shine into his own eyes, giving the clear benefit to Burr.

With ten paces separating the two men, Hamilton asked for a delay to put on his glasses. Looking into the glare of the morning sun, he announced that he was ready. Within a few tense seconds, it would all be over. Two shots exploded the early morning calm. Aaron Burr flinched and stumbled, but it was Alexander Hamilton who had been hit. Though Hamilton lost his life, Aaron

Aaron Burr

Burr's political future also died in that instant.

Burr immediately felt regret. His instinct was to run to Hamilton's side, but he was stopped by his second and rushed to the boat that would row him back to shore. Hamilton knew his wound was mortal; he had been hit just above his hip bone leaving a two-inch entry wound. The bullet ricocheted off a rib and punctured his liver, lodging into his spine. He mumbled a few words and lost consciousness. Hamilton died the next day in Greenwich Village and was buried in the Trinity Church yard in Manhattan.

The difference in background between these two men was deep and wide. Aaron Burr had been born into privilege. His father had been president of the College of New Jersey, which would later be renamed Princeton. Unfortunately, he died the year after Burr was born, and his mother died soon after that. He was a young man when the war against Britain broke out and he became a colonel in the Revolutionary War.

In 1775, he took part in Benedict Arnold's March to Quebec. He served as a lookout at a post outside of Valley Forge during the winter of 1777-1778. In 1779, he resigned his commission because of ill health. General George Washington accepted his resignation, with regret. After leaving the service, he was educated in the field of law. He married a widow 10 years his senior. They had a daughter, and after 12 years of marriage, his wife died.

Alexander Hamilton on the other hand, had been born in the West Indies to a young woman who was not married to his father. He joined the Americans in the Revolution as well, and became the aide-de-camp to General Washington at age 20. Like Aaron Burr, Hamilton spent the winter of 1777-1778 with Washington's Army at Valley Forge. He craved action though, and when he was reprimanded by Washington for some slight, he seized the excuse to resign and get into some real fighting. After the war, Hamilton served in politics and became the first Secretary of the Treasury for the United States. His ideas were controversial, yet progressive. Throughout his short life, he was an outgoing and affable man, positive and extremely intelligent.

The public outcry against Burr over Alexander Hamilton's death was immediate and intense. He hid out until the controversy died out. Though his political life was over, he had a new plan. Burr set out on an extended trip through the South. After spending time with his daughter Theodosia, who was married to the governor of South Carolina, he went to Tennessee to visit his friend Andrew Jackson. He traveled through Alabama, and as a visitor to Huntsville, he was entertained by a prominent family on Eustis Street. He spent a considerable amount of time in New Orleans, and all the while, reports of his activities were being sent back to the White House in Washington.

Rumors began to circulate that he was amassing supplies and men to form a new republic in the southwest. President Jefferson became alarmed that he could be planning to attack the dominion of Spain by taking over Mexico City and establishing himself as the president of a new empire, separate from the eastern United States.

Burr bought land and guns and commissioned to have ships built to carry militia. A warrant was issued for his arrest.

Burr was a fugitive from the federal government. While traveling through Alabama one night in February 1807, he caught the interest of a man in Washington County. Burr and another man had asked for directions to the nearest inn, and although he was disguised in homespun clothing, his fine hand-tooled boots had drawn attention to him. Surprisingly, several people recognized him when they saw him. Aaron Burr was arrested near the Tombigbee River and brought to Richmond, Virginia to stand trial.

On August 3, 1807, his trial began. Luckily for Burr, certain evidence against him was disallowed by the presiding judge. On September 1, he was acquitted of complicity in a plot to establish an empire in the southwest.

From 1808 to 1812, Burr lived in Europe. He returned to live in New York, and his daughter Theodosia Burr Alston, his only child, made plans to visit him at his home. On December 20, 1812, she boarded the schooner *Patriot* in Charleston. The voyage should have taken approximately five days. When two weeks had passed without word from Theodosia or other passengers on the ship, she was assumed lost at sea. There had been a storm off the coast of Nags Head, North Carolina shortly after the ship set sail.

Years later, another explanation was revealed. A man in Alabama confessed that he had been a member of the pirate crew who had boarded the *Patriot* and killed all the passengers. According to his story, and others that later corroborated the tale, Theodosia, dressed entirely in white, was forced to walk the gangplank. She had asked that her father and husband be told of her death, but of course that information would incriminate her killers, and so they never knew her fate. After this story came out, a portrait, believed to be of Theodosia, was discovered in the home of an elderly woman in Nags Head. She said it had been given to her by a member of her family, a known pirate, and that when she had no money to pay her doctor, she offered the oil painting of the beautiful young woman as payment. Members of the Burr family identified Theodosia as the subject of the portrait.

Aaron Burr lived the rest of his life in relative quiet. He married again in 1833, but only lived with his wife for four months. She sued for divorce, and in a strange twist of fate, divorce papers were served to him by the son of Alexander Hamilton, the man he had killed almost 30 years earlier. The divorce was granted on the day of his death, September 14, 1836.

Much has been written about these two men over the last 200 years. Since 1927, Alexander Hamilton's image has graced the U.S. $10 bill, a tribute to the man who was the first Secretary of the Treasury. Legislation was introduced to replace his picture with that of the late President Ronald Reagan, but for now Hamilton will remain.

One of the legends that surrounds Burr's escape from justice is the story that he hid out in The Dismals, a canyon in Franklin County, Alabama. The mysterious name may have been given by a Scotsman to commemorate a craggy spot in Scotland by the same name. One legend says that the musket Aaron Burr used during the American Revolution was found near the cave he used for his campsite.

But the story of Aaron Burr did not end with his death. For years, there have been rumors that his ghost haunted establishments in New York. His ghost was seen in a building that was believed to be his carriage house, or a building built on the property that was his carriage house. According to employees of One if by Land and Two if by Sea on Barrow Street, his ghost has been known to break dishes and pull the chairs out from under unsuspecting patrons. The ghost of a woman, thought to be his daughter Theo, is said to remove the earrings of female diners.

There seems to be a bit of confusion about where exactly the carriage house was. The restaurant claims it was on Barrow Street, yet another source says it was on 3rd Street, approximately 4 blocks away in a nightclub that was known in the 1960s as Café Bizarre. Burr's spirit was contacted by a medium working with author Hans Holzer who has written several books on ghosts. Several people at Café Bizarre had seen the ghost of a man with dark piercing eyes who was wearing a ruffled shirt similar to those worn around the time of the American Revolution. Through the medium, the spirit of Aaron Burr was asking about Theo, his daughter. He would not give his real name, but used one that was a known pseudonym, as well as others that had not been known. Burr had been paranoid in life, with good reason.

He was pleading for someone to find documentation that would clear him as a traitor. He explained where the documentation was, but of course it was long gone.

The spirit alternately pleaded for sympathy, and then got angry. He had been betrayed by a friend and although he would not admit to killing Alexander Hamilton in name, he said he had killed to preserve his honor. There was a female ghost with this Aaron Burr as well, that of his second wife, Betsy Jumel. With the help of the medium, it was believed that Aaron Burr moved on and found peace in the afterworld.

Whether or not these spirits still walk the earth is not really relevant. The story of these two men, whose lives were wasted by a single gunshot, remains as one of the most fascinating tales of American history.

The Sloss Furnace

The city of Birmingham, Alabama owes much of its existence to a man named James Withers Sloss. Sloss was born in Mooresville, Alabama in 1820 to an Irish immigrant father and his wife, whose families were among Alabama's earliest settlers. Sloss was industrious and hard working. At age 15, he took a bookkeeping job in Florence, and later established a country store in nearby Athens, Alabama. Some sources say he was a veteran of the Civil War, though he was given the honorable title "Colonel" before the war.

Sloss and his family moved farther south and he was instrumental in getting the Louisville and Nashville Railroad through the Birmingham community in 1871, helping to establish the thriving town. The cholera epidemic of 1873 dashed the hopes of many of the early financial giants, who gave up and left. The railroad business didn't seem like such a good idea after all; few people traveled and there was nothing for the trains to carry.

That all changed in 1876 when Alabama coke was successfully used to make pig iron. Before that time, iron was made using charcoal from trees, however the devastation from the Civil War left forests in ruins or even non-existent. When the new version of iron was made in 1876 with local coal, it was found to be stronger and even economically more feasible.

Iron could now be made from Alabama's iron ore, using Alabama's coke made from Alabama's coal. This version of iron was not only stronger, but more economic to produce. The first iron was made in 1882, and in 1883, the company won a bronze medal at the Southern Exposition in Kentucky. The industrial center of Alabama was born. In the first year, 14,000 tons of iron was produced. The Pratt Coal and Coke Company was established. It later became the Sloss-Sheffield Furnaces before Sloss sold out in 1889. For nearly 90 years, the Sloss Furnace was a major employer and the towers were etched into Birmingham's skyline. Today, though the workers no longer toil in the relentless heat, it is now a museum to Alabama's industrial past. But it is also known for something else.

Birmingham's Sloss Furnace is known as one of the most haunted places in Alabama. A number of film crews, psychics, and paranormal groups have visited the old furnace and overwhelmingly agree that there is a huge amount of psychic activity there. Since it first opened, the Sloss Furnace, producer of iron ore, attracted many immigrants who would work in less than favorable conditions. Over the years, many were injured, maimed, and over 60 killed in the most heinous manners. Understandably, working in an iron furnace is hard work, but just the slightest mistake can be fatal.

One ghostly legend revolves around a man named Theophilus Calvin Jowers. He worked with the furnaces in unbearable heat, but he loved it. By 1887, he was the assistant foundryman. He was careful, but as he tried to change the bell on a furnace one day, he lost his balance as he walked around the edge. He slipped and fell into the molten iron which quickly claimed him. While his co-workers knew he could not possibly survive the fall into the molten iron, they did try to bring his remains out with a pipe and attached piece of sheet iron. According to the story, they were able to retrieve one shoe, with his foot inside.

Today, visitors report cold spots, orbs, and a most unfriendly energy. They hear disembodied whispers, whistles that are blown mysteriously, and the unmistakable sound of footsteps. Police records indicate over 100 incidents have been reported. And the number of unreported incidents must number in the thousands.

Another similar story involves an especially rough foreman nicknamed Slag. He drove his workers mercilessly, even when they were exhausted. His relentless pushing, combined with their carelessness, caused many deaths during the graveyard shift, which was Slag's reign. Productivity under his rule was high, but it came with a price. One night, Slag himself fell into the molten iron and to his horrible death. Some suggested that it was no accident. Slag's ghostly wanderings have been witnessed by many who see his horribly burned face, contorted with anger. One man claims to have been confronted and then beaten by Slag. When examined after the incident, the man was found to have fist-sized burns all over him. Others have seen the actual ghosts, including that of a man who appears to walk through the sparks of intense heat.

Will the ghosts of the Sloss Furnace ever find peace? Perhaps not. Former workers who lived through their time spent at the Sloss Furnace have described it as a hell on earth.

About the Author

Jacquelyn Procter Gray is the author of several books and numerous short stories. She is editor of *The Huntsville Historical Review*, *Tennessee Valley Leaves*, and associate editor of *Old Tennessee Valley Magazine*. She is the interim curator of the Donnell House in Athens, Alabama and teaches history via distance learning through Early Works Museum in Huntsville. She is a native of Las Vegas, New Mexico and graduate of New Mexico Highlands University.

9 781425 953409